UNDERSTANDING AND RESPONDING TO ECONOMIC ABUSE

FEMINIST DEVELOPMENTS IN VIOLENCE AND ABUSE

Series Editors: Dr Hannah Bows, Durham University (UK) and Professor Nicole Westmarland, Durham University (UK)

Feminist Developments in Violence and Abuse provides a feminist forum for academic work that pushes forward existing knowledge around violence and abuse, informing policy and practice, with the overarching objective of contributing towards ending violence and abuse within our society. The series enables academics, practitioners, policymakers and professionals to continually build and explore their understanding of the dynamics, from the micro- to the macro-level, that are driving violence and abuse. The study of abuse and violence has a large scope for co-producing research, and this series is a home for research involving a broad range of stakeholders; particularly those working in grassroots domestic and sexual violence organisations, police, prosecutors, lawyers, campaign groups, housing and victim services. As violence and abuse research reaches across disciplinary boundaries, the series has an interdisciplinary scope with research impact at the heart.

Available Volumes

Victims' Experiences of the Criminal Justice Response to Domestic Abuse: Beyond Glass Walls
Emma Forbes

Understanding and Responding to Economic Abuse
Nicola Sharp-Jeffs

Forthcoming Volumes

Rape Myths: Causes, Effects, and Societal Contexts
Sofia Persson and Katie Dhingra

Not Your Usual Suspect: Older Offenders of Violence and Abuse
Hannah Bows

Gendered Justice? How Women's Attempts to Cope With, Survive, or Escape Domestic Abuse Can Drive Them into Crime
Jo Roberts

'Rough Sex' and the Criminal Law: Global Perspectives
Hannah Bows and Jonathan Herring

UNDERSTANDING AND RESPONDING TO ECONOMIC ABUSE

BY

NICOLA SHARP-JEFFS
Surviving Economic Abuse (SEA), UK
London Metropolitan University, UK

United Kingdom – North America – Japan – India
Malaysia – China

Emerald Publishing Limited
Howard House, Wagon Lane, Bingley BD16 1WA, UK

First edition 2022

Copyright © 2022 Nicola Sharp-Jeffs. Published under exclusive licence by Emerald Publishing Limited.

Reprints and permissions service
Contact: permissions@emeraldinsight.com

No part of this book may be reproduced, stored in a retrieval system, transmitted in any form or by any means electronic, mechanical, photocopying, recording or otherwise without either the prior written permission of the publisher or a licence permitting restricted copying issued in the UK by The Copyright Licensing Agency and in the USA by The Copyright Clearance Center. No responsibility is accepted for the accuracy of information contained in the text, illustrations or advertisements. The opinions expressed in these chapters are not necessarily those of the Author or the publisher.

British Library Cataloguing in Publication Data
A catalogue record for this book is available from the British Library

ISBN: 978-1-80117-421-3 (Print)
ISBN: 978-1-80117-418-3 (Online)
ISBN: 978-1-80117-420-6 (Epub)

INVESTOR IN PEOPLE

This book is dedicated to victim-survivors of economic abuse. Thank you for trusting me and sharing your experiences. It is written in memory of Rachel Griffin and Stephen Knafler QC.

CONTENTS

List of Figures and Tables	xi
Abbreviations	xiii
Note on Use of Term Victim-Survivor	xv
About the Author	xvii
Foreword	xviii
Preface	xxi
Acknowledgements	xxv
Introduction: 'Rediscovering' Economic Abuse	1

Part One
Understanding Economic Abuse

Chapter One: The 'Technology' of Economic Abuse	23
Chapter Two: How Economic Abuse Is Experienced	71

Part Two
Responding to Economic Abuse

Chapter Three: The Coordinated Community Response Model	103
Chapter Four: Practice Responses to Economic Abuse	121

Chapter Five: Future Directions in Responding to
               Economic Abuse   163

References   175
Index   199

LIST OF FIGURES AND TABLES

FIGURES

Figure One:	The Duluth Power and Control Wheel (DAIP, 1984)	2
Figure Two:	The Economic Power and Control Wheel (Sharp, 2008)	38
Figure Three:	Post-separation Economic Power and Control (Glinski, 2021)	64

TABLES

Table One:	The Scale of Economic Abuse (SEA) (Adams et al., 2008)	26
Table Two:	SEA-12 (Postmus et al., 2016)	28
Table Three:	SEA-2 (Adams et al., 2019)	30
Table Four:	Examples of Preventing Resource Acquisition, Use and Maintenance (Sharp & Learmonth, 2017)	47
Table Five:	Targets of Control	58

CASE STUDY

Case Study One:	Natalie's Story – Economic Abuse in the Context of Coercive Control	35
Case Study Two:	Amy's Story – Creating Economic Dependency	49

Case Study Three:	Annie's Story – Creating Economic Insecurity	51
Case Study Four:	Jean's Story – Written by Her Daughter (Predatory Marriage)	55
Case Study Five:	Layla's Story – Economic Abuse Post-separation	61
Case Study Six:	Emily's Story – Told by Her Dad (Economic Control After Fatal Domestic Abuse)	65
Case Study Seven:	Joy's Story – Socio-economic Status	95
Case Study Eight:	Rosie's Story – Coerced Debt	130
Case Study Nine:	Tom's Story – The Impact on Children	144
Case Study Ten:	Joy's Story – Privately Owned Housing	148

BEST PRACTICE EXAMPLE

Best Practice Example One: Developing a CCR Approach that Embeds Economic Abuse	115
Best Practice Example Two: Embedding Money/Debt Advice into Domestic Abuse Services	134
Best Practice Example Three: Integrating Specialist Knowledge	135
Best Practice Example Four: Domestic Abuse Matters Change Programme	146
Best Practice Example Five: The Whole Housing Approach	150
Best Practice Example Six: An Example of a Specialist Banking Response	155
Best Practice Example Seven: Economic Support Packages for Employees	160

ABBREVIATIONS

AAFDA	Advocacy After Fatal Domestic Abuse
AFV	Adult family violence
BEIS	Business, Energy and Industrial Strategy
CCB	Controlling or coercive behaviour
CCR	Coordinated community response
CSEW	Crime Survey for England and Wales
CWASU	Child and Woman Abuse Studies Unit
CMS	Child Maintenance Service
DAFA	Domestic and Financial Abuse team (LBG)
DAME	Domestic Abuse and Money Education
DAPOs	Domestic Abuse Protection Orders
DASH	Domestic Abuse, Stalking and Honour-based Violence
DCMS	Department for Digital, Culture, Media and Sport
DEAP	Domestic and Economic Abuse Project
DHR	Domestic Homicide Review
DRO	Debt Relief Order
EAEF	Economic Abuse Evidence Form
EDAC	Employers Domestic Abuse Covenant
CPS	Crown Prosecution Service
EVAW	End Violence Against Women
FGM	Female genital mutilation
GVA	Gender Violence Andabuse
HBV	Honour based violence
IDVAs	Independent Domestic Violence Advisors

IPV	Intimate partner violence
LBG	Lloyds Banking Group
MAP	Money Advice Plus
MaPS	Money and Pensions Service
MARACs	Multi-agency risk assessment conferences
MAT	Money Advice Trust
NAB	National Australia Bank
ONS	Office for National Statistics
PSHE	Personal, Social, Health and Economic
RIC	Risk Identification Checklist
SEA	Surviving Economic Abuse (charity)
SEA	Scale of economic abuse (measurement)
SDVC	Specialist Domestic Violence Courts
STADA	Standing Together Against Domestic Abuse
SRE	Sex and Relationships Education
UK	United Kingdom
UN	United Nations
US	United States of America
VAWG	Violence against women and girls
WHA	Whole Housing Approach

NOTE ON USE OF TERM VICTIM-SURVIVOR

The combined term victim-survivor is used to acknowledge that anyone who is experiencing abuse is already surviving what they are in. The term 'victim' can be useful and even empowering when someone is trying to access justice, for example, in court. Some people feel the term 'victim' validates their experience and reassures them that the perpetrator's actions were not their fault. However, other people dislike the term 'victim' because they feel it is disempowering or makes them appear vulnerable. For this reason, when the term 'victim-survivor' cannot be used, the term 'survivor' is used over 'victim'.

ABOUT THE AUTHOR

Dr **Nicola Sharp-Jeffs** OBE is an expert in economic abuse as it occurs within the context of coercive control and has worked in the Violence Against Women and Girls Sector since 2006. She undertook a Churchill Fellowship in 2016 which made her determined to ensure that women in the UK had access to the same innovative policy and practice responses to economic abuse that she witnessed internationally. She set-up the charity Surviving Economic Abuse in 2017 and is its CEO. In 2018, she was also appointed an Emeritus Fellow of the Child and Woman Abuse Studies Unit, London Metropolitan University where, 10 years earlier, she undertook her first piece of research on economic abuse as part of the MA in Woman and Child Abuse.

FOREWORD

Writing a foreword is always a pleasure because the invitation tends to be based on a connection you have with the author and/or the subject, in this case it is both. I have accompanied Nicola as she has developed her knowledge and expertise on economic abuse through shared projects initially and more recently as a supporter of the work of Surviving Economic Abuse, the charity she founded in 2017. This book is a distillation of all she has learnt and how that learning can be used in policy and practice to enable survivors to establish economic security as they rebuild their lives.

As I read the introduction, the word 'rediscovery' led me to reflect on how women's economic dependence has been a core theme in the history of most women's movements. At the turn of the nineteenth century, feminists in many places were writing and campaigning on these issues – they understood that without paid employment or access to financial resources women would remain dependent on their fathers and/or husbands, it was part, alongside suffrage and other issues, of what locked them in the position of second class citizens. The early campaigns for family allowance (later to become child benefit) were rooted in a recognition that women did not have control over household finances and to pay this to mothers made it more likely that it would indeed benefit children. Throughout the twentieth century, women's economic independence was also folded into campaigns on divorce, inheritance, access to education and to the professions. Equal pay, equal education and employment and the right to financial and legal independence were three of the seven demands of the UK Women's Liberation Movement in the 1970s. This issue has, therefore, been at the heart of work on women's equality for a very long time.

The connection with intimate partner violence has also been evident for more than a century. Linda Gordon, in her classic *Heroes of Their Own Lives,* examines the records of a social work agency in Boston, USA, from 1880 to 1960. She documents the gendered conflicts over household income that often sparked men's violence – men saw their wages as theirs, and that they had a right to spend it on themselves and their public lives, women contended that feeding and clothing children should have a prior claim. These connections were also made in the 1980s in the Power and Control wheel, one spoke of which names economic abuse alongside another termed male privilege.

Legacies of these longstanding gendered norms and practices remain, but perhaps have become hidden in plain sight which might be part of the explanation as to why it has taken until the last decade for economic abuse to be explicitly recognised in English speaking research, law, policy and practice. This book not only documents this process but also seeks to clarify language and definitions, to make the multiple layers of economic abuse within coercive control visible. Naming has always had a key role in work on violence against women and girls as the words we use seek to better reflect and encompass experiential realities. One tension that is carefully explored in these pages is the conflation of intimate partner violence and family violence in recent government policy. Whilst extending protections this has been at the expense of clarity and an evidence base – what we know, including about economic abuse, is predominantly from research and practice on partnership relationships and the patriarchal legacies embedded within them. This book makes clear that there is more work to be done exploring the reach of economic abuse into other familial settings and relationships.

Another concept which resonated for me was that of hierarchies of harm, something my PhD research which became *Surviving Sexual Violence* also explored. Law tends to emphasise physical violence, prioritising it in terms of serious harm. But economic abuse challenges such simplistic formulations: it is the aspect of coercive control that most often continues or even increases post-separation and has the potential to undermine victim-survivors efforts to rebuild their lives. This is but another example of how we need to think not just about safety but also freedom when assessing the impacts of both domestic abuse and responses to it. The practice implications of addressing economic abuse have brought new partners and institutions into the coordinated community response and this book highlights some of the ways in which the finance sector can expand the space for action of victim-survivors: the next challenge is how they might narrow that of perpetrators.

Professor Liz Kelly

PREFACE

For many years, economic abuse has been an 'invisible' form of coercive and controlling behaviour. I would raise my hand during discussions about domestic abuse and ask, 'but what about economic abuse?'. It was incomprehensible to me that, when economic abuse threaded through every conversation I had with victim-survivors, these experiences were not reflected within the research literature or policy and practice responses. It was this that led me to explore the different forms of economic abuse and its impact on women and children experiencing domestic abuse within my MA dissertation in Woman and Child Abuse at the Child and Woman Abuse Studies Unit (CWASU), London Metropolitan University back in 2008. I set up a website (www.survivingeconomicabuse.org) and created a Twitter account (@SEAresource) to share and add to the research literature and resources I'd collected.

In 2013, I embarked on a research career at CWASU and sought opportunities to continue building the evidence base. These included: exploring women's economic space for action within a longitudinal piece of research on how women rebuild their lives after domestic abuse; a literature review on financial abuse for the charity Refuge in partnership with The Cooperative Bank; and the first piece of research on the prevalence of financial abuse. My Professional Doctorate (2011–2016) explored the economic safety of young people going missing within the context of forced marriage and child sexual exploitation.

When I heard about the Churchill Fellowship from Claire Lilley and Carlene Firmin (fellow Professional Doctorate students), I was excited by the prospect of witnessing first-hand the innovative practice and policy responses to economic abuse that I was aware of in the USA and Australia. Having successfully applied to the scheme and undertaken my travels, I returned to the UK in late 2016 determined that women should have access to the same responses that I had witnessed. In early 2017, I wrote up my Fellowship report and made recommendations on how this learning could be applied in the UK context. I decided to be the change I wanted to see and so started the process of setting up the charity Surviving Economic Abuse (SEA).

By June 2017, SEA was registered with the Charity Commission and had been awarded a grant from the Tampon Tax Fund administered by the Department for Digital, Culture, Media and Sport (DCMS). The charity's founding Economic Justice Project was inspired by practice I had seen in the USA on responding to coerced debt.

During this time, I also discovered that the three-year Domestic Abuse Money Education (DAME) Project set up by Women's Aid in partnership with Money Advice Plus (MAP) in 2010 had been continued by MAP. We embarked on a new partnership (which is now twice award-winning) and were awarded a second Tampon Tax grant to continue to deliver a national casework service for victims of domestic abuse experiencing financial difficulty. Together we also provided training on economic abuse to other money and debt advice services as well as domestic abuse and housing services around the country. With top-up money from the Home Office, the Domestic and Economic Abuse Project (DEAP) expanded to provide a national support service to banks and building societies, and a resource and information function to develop 'Tools to Support' for professionals and 'Tools to Thrive' for victim-survivors.

Four years later, SEA has grown to a team of 20+ with a clear mission – to raise awareness of economic abuse and to transform responses to it. It would not have been possible to write this book four years ago, but the impact of our work and the support we have received for it means that much has changed.

SEA successfully called on the Westminster Government to both name and define economic abuse within the Domestic Abuse Act (2021). The charity went on to work with peers and academic Dr Cassandra Wiener to secure an amendment to the Serious Crime Act (2015), extending the controlling or coercive behaviour offence in an intimate or family relationship to apply post-separation. These legislative developments have, in turn, created a framework within which to respond.

Interest in economic abuse as a vulnerable customer issue has also grown during this time. In 2017, I was part of an advisory group to UK Finance which developed a Code of Practice, setting out principles that banks and building societies should adhere to when responding to financial abuse. Thirty UK Finance members are now signed up to the newly refreshed 2021 Financial Abuse Code.[1]

SEA held its inaugural 'Banking on Change' conference in December 2018, and we invited Norm Kalcovski of National Australia Bank (NAB) to share his pioneering work to address economic abuse. Having met Norm on my Fellowship travels I knew there was no-one better to make the case for change. I am particularly proud of the partnership SEA has gone on to establish with Lloyds Banking Group (LBG), helping them set up and train a specialist Domestic and Financial Abuse Team (DAFA), to which a member of the SEA team is now seconded.

Throughout this time, I have continued to undertake and publish research on economic abuse as an Emeritus Fellow at

CWASU, including a multi-country study with international academics. This reviewed and analysed the global literature on economic abuse to determine how it is defined and what measures are used to capture its prevalence and impact. Just 46 peer-reviewed articles (with a full or partial quantitative focus) were identified, leading us to observe that this was 'considerably small in comparison to the number of articles that would likely be identified in a global review focussed on physical or sexual violence' (Postmus, Hoge, Breckenridge, Sharp-Jeffs, & Chung, 2018, p. 277).

I remember Professor Liz Kelly, Director of Child and Woman Abuse Studies Unit (CWASU), telling me how, when she wrote *Surviving Sexual Violence* in 1988 there were very few books related to this issue on the library bookshelf. Today there are many. This book, therefore, reflects my own efforts to see economic abuse researched and recognised in the same way.

It is published at a time when economic abuse has never been so high within the public consciousness and on the political agenda. Abusers used the conducive context created by Covid-19 to establish and/or extend their control over their current or former partners' economic resources. The response to the pandemic also compounded existing economic inequalities, as Covid-19 safety measures had a disproportionate impact on women. Yet despite all the challenges that the pandemic created, it has also been a time where we have seen extraordinary innovation in responses to the issue. As Chapter Five recognises, it is vital that we keep this momentum going.

ACKNOWLEDGEMENTS

This book has taken years to research and so there are many people to thank!

First and foremost, the victim-survivors to whom this book is dedicated. It is their strength and survival that fuels my passion – working towards a day when all women are safe and achieve their full potential.

The women of the CWASU including my peers at London Metropolitan University set me on my feminist and academic path. A particular thank you to Professor Liz Kelly for the unwavering belief, support, and encouragement she has shown me.

To all the women I work alongside in the violence against women and girls' sector as well as the women and men across the financial services sector – both nationally and internationally. You inspire me every day and I cannot thank you enough for your support. A special shout out to Jeanette Hope and Karen Perrier at MAP and Jane Rodrick and Fiona Cannon at LBG.

I am immensely privileged and proud to have grown a team at SEA whose expertise on different aspects of economic abuse has now outgrown mine. Alongside Experts by Experience and a committed board of Trustees, advisory group members and ambassadors, we work together to raise awareness of economic abuse and transform responses to it. I hope that this book goes some way towards us achieving our mission.

I met my husband, Neil, through his pro bono work in support of a supreme court challenge on whether the term 'domestic abuse' encompassed emotional and financial abuse. Fortunately, he won! I will be forever grateful that this work brought us together. He is my biggest supporter.

Lastly, and certainly not least, thank you to my family and friends for making space in their lives for my obsession with' all things economic abuse'. Friends and colleagues Janqui Mehta, Lisa King, Gudrun Burnet, Nicole Jacobs, Richard Walsh, Nesta Lloyd-Jones, Emma Scott, Jo Youle and Holly Cameron are a constant source of support.

NOTE

1. 2021 Financial Abuse Code | UK Finance.

INTRODUCTION: 'REDISCOVERING' ECONOMIC ABUSE

Lack of control over income and other economic resources has a profound impact on victim-survivors of domestic abuse. It is commonly given as the reason why they are unable to leave an abuser (Lyon, 2002, p. 12), forcing many to stay for longer than they want and so experiencing more injuries as a result (Earlywhite & Stohl, 2005). Economic insecurity post-separation is also one of the reasons why many victim-survivors say they have no option but to return to an abuser (Aguirre, 1985; Davis, 1999; Lyon, 2002; Wilcox, 2006).

In this way, economic security underpins physical safety. Research by Walby and Allen (2004) has shown that women are three and a half times more likely to be subject to domestic violence if they find it impossible to find £100 at short notice. When physical and sexual domination is exerted alongside rigid control of a woman's movements, sociability, money, food and working life then she is at increased risk of homicide (Websdale, 1999). Moreover, the experience of economic abuse is positively correlated with suicide (Aitken & Munro, 2018).

THE DULUTH POWER AND CONTROL WHEEL

Victim-survivors identified control over economic resources as a tactic used by perpetrators of domestic abuse in the 1980s, introducing the term 'economic abuse' into discourse through the Duluth Power and Control Wheel (DAIP, 1984).

Yet, over the years, economic abuse has received little attention in research, policy or practice. This book is part of the process of 'rediscovering' economic abuse. It provides an understanding of economic abuse and considers best practice responses.

Figure One. The Duluth Power and Control Wheel (DAIP, 1984).

Source: Domestic Abuse Intervention, 202 East Superior Street, Duluth, Minnesota 55802, 218-722-2781, www.theduluthmodel.org.

FINANCIAL OR ECONOMIC ABUSE?

In the UK context, the term financial abuse has been used to describe an abuser's control of money and finances (see Chapter One). However, as Littwin (2012) observes, this does not capture the control of economic resources (such as food, telephones, transport) more broadly. Thus, whilst money is central to both (Singh, 2022) and they involve similar behaviours, Sharp-Jeffs (2015a) argues that financial abuse is best understood as a 'sub-category' of economic abuse and that using the more inclusive term better recognises the range of behaviours that abusers use to control their partners. For this reason, the terms financial abuse and economic abuse should not be used interchangeably.

RECOGNITION OF ECONOMIC (INCLUDING FINANCIAL) ABUSE IN RESEARCH

Domestic abuse continues to be predominantly associated with physical abuse so that there is less recognition of 'non-physical' forms of abuse. Westmarland (2015) observed that financial abuse was 'probably the least researched area of partner violence, with very little academic literature on the topic' (p. 40). Similarly, a multi-country study in 2018 identified just 46 peer-reviewed articles with a full or partial quantitative focus on economic abuse, leading the authors to observe that this was 'considerably small in comparison to the number of articles that would likely be identified in a global review focused on physical or sexual violence' (Postmus, Hoge, Breckenridge, Sharp-Jeffs, & Chung, 2018, p. 277). At the same time, economic abuse has historically been conceptualised as a form of emotional abuse within research studies (Loring, 1994). This resulted in a lack of definitional clarity, making it difficult to measure whether policy and practice responses were responding to economic abuse appropriately (Sharp-Jeffs, 2021a), if indeed, at all.

It is only recently that researchers have turned their attention to understanding and measuring economic abuse. Through developing the scale of economic abuse, Adams, Sullivan, Bybee, and Greeson (2008) were able to provide statistical evidence that economic abuse is a distinct construct. Outlaw (2009) argues that it is important to disaggregate forms of 'non-physical' abuse in this way since they may have different trajectories and vary both in prevalence and their relationship to physical violence.

Adams and her colleagues also developed a definition of economic abuse which is now widely used within academia and, as Chapter One discusses, forms the basis of the definition used within the Domestic Abuse Act (2021). Economic abuse:

> *Involves behaviours that control a person's ability to acquire, use, or maintain economic resources, thus threatening their economic security and potential for self-sufficiency. (Adams et al., 2008, p. 564)*

RECOGNITION OF ECONOMIC ABUSE IN POLICY AND LEGISLATION

In 2005 the Westminster Government introduced a cross-governmental policy definition of domestic violence:

> *Any incident of threatening behaviour, violence or abuse [psychological, physical, sexual, financial or emotional] between adults who are or have been intimate partners or family members, regardless of gender or sexuality. (Home Office, 2005, p. 7)*

This followed calls from women's groups for an integrated strategy to deal with violence against women (Kelly & Westmarland, 2014). Whilst not a statutory or legal definition, agencies were expected to adhere to it. A Supreme Court judgement handed down in January 2011[1] reinforced that the term 'domestic violence' had come to acquire a meaning beyond physical violence only, and that it should be interpreted to include the use of emotional, psychological or financial abuse.

In March 2011, the Westminster Government committed to consult on a revised definition of domestic violence in response to a recommendation made by the Home Affairs Committee following its inquiry into domestic violence, including so-called 'honour' killings, and forced marriage (House of Commons, 2008). In September 2012, it was announced that the Government definition would be expanded to include those aged 16–17 and wording changed to reflect the concept of coercive control (Home Office/AVA, 2013). The new definition stated that domestic violence was:

> *Any incident or pattern of incidents of controlling, coercive or threatening behaviour, violence or abuse between those aged 16 or over who are or have been intimate partners or family members regardless of gender or sexuality. This can encompass, but is not limited to, the following types of abuse:*
>
> - *psychological*
> - *physical*
> - *sexual*
> - *financial*
> - *emotional*

> *Controlling behaviour is a range of acts designed to make a person subordinate and/or dependent by isolating them from sources of support, exploiting their resources and capacities for personal gain, depriving them of the means needed for independence, resistance and escape and regulating their everyday behaviour.*
>
> *Coercive behaviour is an act or a pattern of acts of assault, threats, humiliation and intimidation or other abuse that is used to harm, punish, or frighten their victim. (Home Office/AVA, 2013, p. 2)*

Because the definition applied to policy development only, the new emphasis on coercive control did not create a change in the law. This meant that there was no way of holding perpetrators to account for the full spectrum of their behaviour via the criminal justice system. Westmarland (2015, p. 5) observed that this was 'more the case for some forms of financial and psychological abuse than for physical and sexual violence'. It was not until the offence of controlling or coercive behaviour (CCB) in an intimate or family relationship was introduced within section 76 of the Serious Crime Act (2015) that the gap in the law was closed.

However, despite it being widely acknowledged that the new offence of CCB provided a framework through which to understand and address emotional/psychological abuse, there was no recognition at the time that it would also act as a mechanism through which to better respond to financial abuse, or economic abuse more broadly (Sharp-Jeffs & Learmonth, 2017). Indeed, the Westminster Government's four-year *Ending Violence Against Women and Girls (VAWG) strategy* published in March 2016 made just one reference to financial abuse – within a case study example (HM Government, 2016). The issue itself was not addressed within the strategy, nor the action plan that underpinned it. Reference was made only to the fact that the needs of victims may be 'complex' and can include 'assistance with debt'.

THE DOMESTIC ABUSE ACT (2021)

In 2017, the Westminster Government announced its intention to bring forward new domestic abuse legislation which would introduce a statutory definition of domestic abuse. From the outset, the Surviving Economic Abuse (SEA) charity called on the Westminster Government to take the opportunity this provided to adopt the 'more inclusive' concept (Christy, Welter, Dundon, & Bruce, 2020, p. 3) by replacing the term financial abuse with economic abuse.

This call was consistent with the United Nations (UN) General Assembly's (2002) resolution on the elimination of violence against women which recognises that 'domestic violence can include economic deprivation'[2] and the UN Secretary General's (2006) in-depth study on violence against women which states that economic abuse and exploitation are manifestations of violence 'that require greater visibility and attention' (p. 47). Similarly, the 2011 Council of Europe Convention on preventing and combatting violence against women and domestic violence (the Istanbul Convention) recognises that all acts of gender-based violence result in, or are likely to result in, physical, sexual, psychological or economic harm or suffering to women (Article 3b). More specifically, the Convention's definition of domestic violence is understood to mean all acts of physical, sexual, psychological or economic violence that occur within the family or domestic unit (Article 3c; Council of Europe, 2011).

Research by Sharp-Jeffs and Learmonth (2017) drew attention to the fact that economic abuse is more likely to be experienced within the context of coercive control than not. An analysis of successfully prosecuted cases of the CCB offence revealed that 6 in 10 cases featured at least one form of economic abuse – a finding which has remained broadly consistent in the intervening years (Sharp-Jeffs, Royal, & Gibson, forthcoming). But none of the newspaper reports which were analysed and outlined these behaviours named nor recognised them as such.

Inclusion of economic abuse within the statutory definition was supported by victim-survivors and the women's sector at each stage of the Act's development (Sharp-Jeffs, 2021a). In March 2018, the consultation document *Transforming the Response to Domestic Abuse* proposed including economic abuse within the new statutory definition of domestic abuse and, when the draft Bill was published in late January 2019, economic abuse was both named and defined within it. In the paper published alongside the Bill, the Westminster Government explicitly recognised that economic abuse 'encompasses a wider range of behaviours than financial abuse' (HM Government, 2019, p. 6). Furthermore, the term 'economic abuse' was used 35 times within the paper and 7 commitments addressing economic abuse were outlined within its plan of action moving forward.[3]

In addition to successfully influencing the Westminster Government to both name and define economic abuse within the Bill, SEA worked with Labour peer Baroness Lister, academic Dr Cassandra Wiener and Conservative peers Baroness Bertin and Baroness Sanderson on an amendment to the Serious Crime Act (2015), again with the support of the VAWG sector, including the charity SafeLives. This sought to extend the CCB offence in an intimate or family relationship to apply post-separation. On 1 March 2021, the Government accepted the proposed amendment, meaning that ongoing economic abuse and other forms of coercive control can be prosecuted when the victim-survivor is no longer living with and/or in a relationship with the abuser. The Domestic Abuse Bill finally became the Domestic Abuse Act on 29 April 2021.

RECOGNITION OF ECONOMIC ABUSE IN PRACTICE

Given the focus of second wave feminism on financial independence for women (Westmarland, 2015), it is perplexing that work to address financial abuse was described in 2008 as 'under-funded and overlooked' by the VAWG sector (Kail, Blathwayt, & Jarvinen, 2008, p. 42). Whilst charities such as Refuge and Women's Aid went on to develop their own materials and launched initiatives to address this gap (Advice Development Project, ADP, 2003; Barron, 2012; Refuge, 2008a) such efforts focussed on individual advocacy and did not have the national reach needed to create systems change. In 2016, the End Violence Against Women (EVAW) coalition observed a continued lack of focus on women's economic rights (Dustin, 2016) and Sharp-Jeffs (2016a, p. 35) noted that, when compared to international practice, responses to financial abuse in the UK remained at an 'early stage of development'.

Reflecting the development of research literature on the different aspects of domestic abuse, Sharp-Jeffs (2016a) suggests that economic (including financial) abuse has come last on a continuum of intervention – leading on from practice responses which initially focussed on physical abuse and then sexual and emotional abuse. A scoping study on economic abuse across three London Boroughs in 2017, for example, found that few professionals working in the domestic abuse sector had received training on economic abuse and there was no proactive screening for economic abuse. As such prevalence was unknown and support needs were unclear (Surviving Economic Abuse (SEA), 2017).

In many ways, economic abuse has been viewed as a 'lesser' form of violence or at the bottom of a hierarchy of harm. Due to funding pressures and commissioning models, domestic abuse services have had little alternative but to focus on reducing immediate risk of physical harm rather than the role economic security plays in preventative work and long-term safety (SEA, 2020). Radford and Tsutsumi (2004) assert that whilst 'risk discourse' in the domestic violence sphere has been useful in uncovering violence and getting it taken seriously, it has also meant rationing strategies to those who are deemed 'most at risk' thus denying protection to the majority.

A FRAMEWORK WITHIN WHICH TO RESPOND

The 'rediscovery' of economic abuse within the Domestic Abuse Act has provided a framework within which to respond.

Raising Awareness

The Westminster Government stated that it wanted to ensure that victims of economic abuse can be identified and supported. In support of this commitment, funding was made available via grants to help professionals recognise economic abuse in a range of different contexts, including policing, financial capability work and within the financial services industry (see Chapter Four).

This is vital, since not all victim-survivors will recognise that they are experiencing economic abuse. Indeed, for many years, it has been widely assumed that economic resources are shared equitably within a household meaning that their use as a source of power has rarely been recognised (Branigan, 2004; Green & Pearce, 2002; Westaway & McKay, 2007). In

2015, for example, a survey undertaken by Citizen's Advice found that only 39% of surveyed adults were aware that financial abuse is a form of domestic violence.[4] When a representative sample of women aged 18–21 across England were asked if 'taking your money' was a form of domestic violence, almost half the sample disagreed (Refuge, 2008b; see also YWCA, 2009). In addition, only two in five of financial abuse victim-survivors questioned within a nationally representative survey stated that they had recognised it from the outset (Sharp-Jeffs, 2015b).

Research undertaken for SEA found that awareness activity linked to the Domestic Abuse Bill enabled victim-survivors to understand and name their experiences (Kelly, 2020).

> *I heard a piece on Radio 4's Money Box programme, where SEA was mentioned as well as the phrase economic abuse. Before that, I didn't have the language for it.*

> *When I learned that the Domestic Violence Bill included what was termed economic abuse. I felt relieved and not alone, or that I had done something wrong.*

Anecdotally, the charity MAP observes that it was rare for women in contact with their national casework service to name economic abuse prior to 2017, but that since the announcement of the new legislation, this has changed as awareness of the issue has grown.

Holding Perpetrators to Account

Part of any response to domestic abuse must be holding perpetrators to account (see Chapter Three). Naming economic abuse within the statutory definition does not criminalise economic abuse in and of itself. However, the Westminster Government has updated relevant legal guidance for prosecutors to ensure cases involving economic abuse can be successfully prosecuted where appropriate. This includes updating the statutory guidance for the offence of CCB to include references to economic abuse and a commitment to include economic abuse in the statutory guidance for future Stalking Protection Orders and Domestic Abuse Protection Orders (DAPOs, Home Office, 2019).

MEASURING NATIONAL PREVALENCE

The Crime Survey for England and Wales (CSEW) measures the national prevalence of financial abuse, but not economic abuse since the question asked focusses only on household money. Moreover, the Office for National Statistics (ONS) does not present the CSEW findings on financial abuse separately. Instead, they are grouped under the heading 'non-physical' forms of domestic abuse, alongside the answer to a question on emotional abuse.[5]

The most recent figures (in the year to March 2020) from the ONS show that 12.2% of adults have experienced non-physical (financial and emotional) abuse from a partner/family member since the age of 16 and 3.6% of adults aged 16–74 in the last year (Stripe, 2020). Yet, even if the ONS did report the findings on financial abuse separately, they should be treated cautiously, since the question posed on financial abuse is subjective, asking whether someone has prevented them from having their 'fair share' of the household money.

To fill this gap, a nationally representative survey was undertaken by The Cooperative Bank and Refuge in 2015 (Sharp-Jeffs, 2015b) and updated in 2020 (Butt, 2020). In the more recent survey, around one in six (16%) respondents stated that they had experienced economic abuse from a current or former partner, although in both surveys it is noted that the actual numbers may be higher, with respondents who answered no to experiencing economic abuse going on to indicate that they had experienced economically controlling behaviour via their responses to subsequent questions.

The Istanbul Convention requires State Parties to provide disaggregated data on all forms of violence (physical, sexual, psychological or economic) covered by the scope of the Convention (Walby, 2016). As such, developing an accurate measure for economic abuse is a clear a priority for the Westminster Government. Not only must this measure be objective and capture the multi-faceted nature of economic abuse (Sharp-Jeffs, 2015a), but it must be clear about who is doing what to whom.

DIFFERENT TYPES OF RELATIONSHIP

The statutory definition of domestic abuse within which economic abuse is recognised (see Chapter One) sets out that A (the abuser) and B (the victim-survivor) must be personally connected to each other. The phrase 'personally connected' serves to capture different types of relationships including current/former intimate partners as well as family members.

It has been argued that the conflation of intimate partner violence (IPV) with adult family violence (AFV) causes confusion since it presumes that the dynamics underpinning both are the same (Kelly & Westmarland, 2014) – something which is acknowledged by the Home Office (2013). The evidence base from which responses to domestic abuse have been developed draw on what is known about women's experiences of abuse from a current/former partner within a heterosexual relationship and within the context of coercive control. This understanding is, therefore, gendered (Kelly & Westmarland, 2014).

The Duluth Power and Control Wheel in Figure One illustrates how male privilege underpins current understandings of IPV. Traditional attitudes towards gender roles are made possible by gender inequality and the social and economic advantage that men continue to enjoy. Coercive control is, therefore, a concept that was developed by women 'to make sense of the many subtle and not so subtle ways in which men impose their will in heterosexual relationships' and which 'draws on cultural norms about both masculinity and femininity'. It cannot 'be simply read across into other relationships which are often generational and in which the issues of gender and sexuality play out differently' (Kelly & Westmarland, 2014).

For this reason, economic abuse within the context of an intimate partner relationship will be different to economic abuse experienced in the context of elder abuse (commonly perpetrated by an adult child or carer) which will be different again when it is experienced by a young person being forced into marriage (commonly perpetrated by a family member).

A GENDERED FRAMING OF ECONOMIC ABUSE

A gendered analysis therefore informs the framing of economic abuse in the chapters which follow. In addition to the concept of coercive control (Stark, 2007; see Chapter Two) the related concept of 'space for action' (Kelly, 2003) is important. This term is used to understand the impact of coercive control on a victim-survivors' autonomy or agency.[6] It describes how victim-survivors intentionally and actively narrow their space for action (adapting their behaviour to prevent physical assault based on previous challenge) and/or have it narrowed for them by having to live within parameters set by the perpetrator (Westmarland, 2015).

Wherever possible, research exploring the intersection of gender with other characteristics such as race, class (or socio-economic status), sexuality and disability is shared and explored with respect to the experience of victim-survivors. This serves to highlight the need for further research which increases understanding of how economic abuse is used as a mechanism of control by intimate partners and family members across a range of different contexts.

OUTLINE OF BOOK

This introductory chapter has explained the difference between financial and economic abuses and outlined the reasons why economic abuse requires a distinct response. Through exploring how economic abuse has been 'rediscovered' in research, policy, legislation and practice, the potential of the Domestic Abuse Act (2021) in providing a framework within which stakeholders can respond to victim-survivors and hold perpetrators responsible is clear.

The rest of the book is divided into two sections: understanding economic abuse (Chapters One and Two) and responding to economic abuse (Chapters Three and Four).

Chapter One draws on the available research literature to explore the definition of economic abuse set out in the Westminster Government's Domestic Abuse Act (2021). In so doing, it builds an understanding of the 'technology' or variety of means via which economic abuse is perpetrated (Green & Pearce, 2002) including constructs (restriction, exploitation and sabotage) and the 'targets of control' (Adams, Greeson, Littwin, & Javorka, 2019). This provides insight into how the dynamics of economic abuse not only create economic dependency, but economic insecurity which can also limit economic space for action.

Since the overarching statutory definition of domestic abuse encompasses coercion and control by family members as well as intimate partners, this is addressed with reference to 'single incidents' of economic abuse. However, the focus of this chapter is on economic abuse as a course of conduct. As such, the ongoing nature of economic abuse is outlined, highlighting the challenges associated with victim-survivors having to 'rebuild back' before they can move forward, yet often in the context of ongoing interference through post-separation abuse (SEA, 2018), as well as institutional abuse (Sharp, 2008). Dealing with economic abuse and its legacies is not a linear journey (Kelly, Sharp, & Klein, 2014) so Chapter One also considers how the Domestic Abuse Act (2021) provides a mechanism through which to address this.

Chapter Two considers how economic abuse is experienced by victim-survivors. It starts by exploring how abusers derive their power from structural inequalities linked to gender, socio-economic status, ethnicity, sexuality, disability and age. It recognises that, whilst anyone can experience economic abuse, the likelihood increases when an individual has fewer personal, social and economic resources to draw on. For this reason, individuals who experience intersecting inequalities are at particular risk. Abusers use their power to wear down a victim-survivors' resistance to coercive control through targeting these resources, thereby (further) reducing their space for action. Chapter Two concludes by considering the ripple effect of economic abuse (VonDeLinde & Sussman, 2017) in the short medium and long term. Based on this understanding, responses to economic abuse can then be developed.

Chapter Three argues that the new understanding of economic abuse needs to be translated into policy and practice frameworks. It explores the potential of the coordinated community response (CCR) model to do this, suggesting that it needs to be broadened to embrace 'non-traditional' stakeholders and sectors that have, up until now, been viewed as part of the 'wider support sector' if economic abuse is to be effectively addressed. This will enable the CCR to maximise spaces within which victim-survivors can speak out, ensure that they are supported and hold abusers to account. The chapter ends by outlining the component parts that underpin the CCR and considers how economic abuse can be incorporated into each. This 'sets the scene' for Chapter Four which explores the role of different sectors and stakeholders in more detail.

Chapter Four begins by exploring what economic advocacy is and how its principles can be used to increase a victim-survivors' economic space for action, thereby restoring or creating economic security/safety. These principles are considered within a continuum of advocacy which extends from individual through to institutional. Stakeholder responses within the voluntary, public and private sectors are then considered through this lens, and examples are used to illustrate best practice. For each stakeholder, the link to economic abuse is outlined and practice suggestions are made. Although this section cannot and does not seek to provide an exhaustive list of all stakeholders (there are many), the approaches and interventions used by stakeholders in one context can be 'borrowed' and adapted for use in others. Taken as a whole, this chapter therefore also provides insight into how a range of stakeholders need to contribute to the CCR for it to be successful.

The concluding chapter picks up on the themes raised within the book and explores future directions for research, policy and practice.

NOTES

1. In the case of *Yemshaw* v. *London Borough of Hounslow*.

2. OHCHR | Declaration on the Elimination of Violence against Women.

3. Economic abuse CP15 – Transforming the Response to Domestic Abuse – Consultation Response and Draft Bill – January 2019 (publishing.service.gov.uk).

   1. Include reference to economic abuse in the statutory guidance for the offence of CCB and in the statutory guidance for future Stalking Protection Orders and DAPOs (Home Office).
   2. Update legal guidance for prosecutors to ensure cases of economic abuse can be successfully prosecuted (CPS).
   3. Continue to work with UK Finance to encourage banks and financial authorities to do more to support victims of domestic abuse (Home Office).
   4. Provide £200,000 to the National Skills Academy for Financial Services to develop and deliver financial capability training for front-line workers (Home Office).
   5. Provide funding to update the Domestic Abuse Matters police change programme so that it includes economic abuse (Home Office).
   6. Provide approximately £250,000 of funding to create a national advice service for banks and building societies, increase the capacity of existing telephone casework services for victims of domestic abuse and develop resources to help people identify if they are experiencing economic abuse (Home Office).
   7. Work closely with the Scottish Government to establish the practicalities of delivering split payments in Universal Credit in Scotland (Department for Work and Pensions).

4. Only 2 in 5 people are aware of financial abuse - Citizens Advice.

5. Perhaps reflecting understanding of economic abuse as a form of emotional abuse.

6. Inspired by Lundgren's (1998) earlier work on 'women's life space'.

PART ONE

UNDERSTANDING ECONOMIC ABUSE

Chapter One

THE 'TECHNOLOGY' OF ECONOMIC ABUSE

This chapter draws on the available research literature to explore the definition of economic abuse set out in the Westminster Government's Domestic Abuse Act (2021). In so doing, it builds an understanding of the 'technology' or variety of means via which economic abuse is perpetrated (Green & Pearce, 2002) including constructs (restriction, exploitation and sabotage) and the 'targets of control' (Adams et al., 2019). This will provide insight into how the dynamics of economic abuse not only create economic dependency, but economic insecurity which can also limit economic space for action.

Since the overarching statutory definition of domestic abuse encompasses coercion and control by family members too this is addressed with reference to 'single incidents' of economic abuse. However, the focus of this chapter is on economic abuse as a course of conduct. As such, the ongoing nature of economic abuse is outlined, highlighting the challenges associated with victim-survivors having to 'rebuild back' before they can move forward, yet often in the context of ongoing interference through post-separation abuse (SEA, 2018), as well as institutional abuse (Sharp, 2008). Dealing with economic abuse and its legacies is not a linear journey (Kelly et al., 2014) so this chapter also considers how the Domestic Abuse Act (2021) provides a mechanism through which to address this.

DEFINING DOMESTIC ABUSE WITHIN THE DOMESTIC ABUSE ACT

As outlined in the introductory chapter, practice responses to domestic abuse in England and Wales have historically followed various policy definitions; however, the Domestic Abuse Act (2021) introduced a statutory definition of domestic abuse for the first time – 1(1-3):

> *Behaviour of a person ('A') towards another person ('B') is 'domestic abuse' if (a) A and B are each aged 16 or over and are personally connected to each other, and (b) the behaviour is abusive.*
>
> *Behaviour is 'abusive' if it consists of any of the following – (a) physical or sexual abuse; (b) violent or threatening behaviour; (c) controlling or coercive behaviour; (d) economic abuse; (e) psychological, emotional, or other abuse; and it does not matter whether the behaviour consists of a single incident or a course of conduct.*

The statutory definition sets out that A and B must be personally connected to each other. The phrase 'personally connected' is used to ensure that different types of relationships are captured. As discussed in the introduction, this includes current partners, ex-partners as well as family members.

DEFINING ECONOMIC ABUSE WITHIN THE DOMESTIC ABUSE ACT

The Domestic Abuse Act defines economic abuse at 1(4).[1] The following sections break down the definition of economic abuse to explore what it means in practice.

'Any Behaviour'

> *'Economic abuse' means any behaviour that has a substantial adverse effect on B's ability to (a) acquire, use or maintain money or other property, or (b) obtain goods or services.*

Controlling behaviours that limit women's economic wellbeing have been described within the violence against women literature since the 1970s (Sharp-Jeffs, 2021a). Five of these are captured under the 'using economic abuse' heading within the Duluth Power and Control Wheel (Figure One). They include preventing her from getting or keeping a job; making her ask for money; giving her an allowance; taking her money; and not letting her know about or have access to family income. Except for 'preventing her from getting or keeping a job', these examples are all linked specifically to money and finances.

MEASURING ECONOMIC CONTROL: CONSTRUCTS

Usefully, researchers have sought to develop instruments to measure economic abuse. This means that the behaviours outlined above, and many more besides, can be grouped into constructs.

For instance, in 2008 the Scale of Economic Abuse (SEA) was developed by Adams and her colleagues. Drawing on the research literature and conversations with researchers, advocates and survivors, the US-based researchers generated an initial pool of 120 economically abusive behaviours. This was refined to a 28-item scale through data from a sample of 103 service-users (99% experienced economic abuse) and organised into two statistically distinct constructs: economic control (17 items) and economic exploitation (11 items).

Table One. The Scale of Economic Abuse (SEA) (Adams et al., 2008).

Economic control:

1. Steal the car keys or take the car so you couldn't go look for a job or go to a job interview
2. Do things to keep you from going to your job
3. Beat you up if you needed to go to work
4. Threaten you to make you leave work
5. Demand that you quit your job
6. Do things to keep you from having money of your own
7. Take your pay-check, financial aid check, tax refund, disability payment or other support payments from you
8. Decide how you could spend money rather than letting you spend it how you saw fit
9. Demand to know how money was spent
10. Demand that you give them receipts and/or change when you spent money
11. Keep you from having the money you needed to buy food, clothes or other necessities
12. Hide money so that you could not find it
13. Keep you from having access to your bank accounts

Table One   (Continued)

14. Keep financial information from you
15. Make important financial decisions without talking with you about it first
16. Make you ask for money
17. Threaten you or beat you up for paying the bills or buying things that were needed

Economic exploitation:

18. Take money from your purse, wallet or bank account without your permission and/or knowledge
19. Force you to give them money or let them use your check-book, ATM card or credit card
20. Steal your property
21. Pay bills late or not pay bills that were in your name or both your names
22. Build up debt under your name by doing things like use your credit card or run up the phone bill
23. Refuse to get a job so you had to support your family alone
24. Gamble with your money or your shared money
25. Have you ask your family or friends for money but not let you pay them back
26. Convince you to lend them money but not pay it back
27. Pawn your property or your shared property
28. Spend the money you needed for rent or other bills

Postmus, Plummer, and Stylianou (2016; also in the USA) tested the SEA with 120 women participating in a financial literacy programme for survivors of domestic violence (94% experienced economic abuse). Using factor analysis, they produced a cut down scale of 12-items (SEA-12). Through this process they added 'employment sabotage' to the constructs of economic control and economic exploitation.

Table Two.   SEA-12 (Postmus et al., 2016).

Economic control:

1. Make you ask them for money
2. Demand to know how money was spent
3. Demand that you give them receipts and/or change when you spend money
4. Keep financial information from you
5. Make important financial decisions without talking to you first

Employment sabotage:

6. Threaten you to make you leave work
7. Demand that you quit your job
8. Beat you up if you said you needed to go to work
9. Do things to keep you going to your job

Economic exploitation:

10. Spend the money you need for rent or other bills
11. Pay bills late or not pay bills that were in your name or both your names
12. Build up debt under your name by doing things like using your credit card or run up the phone bill

An analysis of 46 peer-reviewed articles on economic abuse showed that those containing a clear definition mostly drew either on the work of Adams et al. (2008) or Postmus et al. (2016) and that these constructs were conceptually useful: economic control was recognised in 87% (n=40) of the studies, economic exploitation in 70% (n=32) and employment sabotage in 46% (n=21).

Yet, when Adams and colleagues revisited both the SEA and SEA-12 scales they concluded that they had failed to sufficiently reflect the 'function of economic abuse as a mechanism of control' (Adams et al., 2019, p. 269). Both the original and revised scales imply that control applies to a subset of economically abusive behaviours when, in fact, control underlies *all* economically abusive behaviour.

Following the same iterative conceptual and statistical process, the researchers therefore drew on data from 248 women seeking services (96% experienced economic abuse) to create a 14-item scale (SEA-2) which reflects a two-dimensional conceptualisation of control:

- *Economic restriction* is described as limiting access to and use of economic resources, thereby forcibly establishing an arrangement in which the victim is dependent on the abuser for financial and material resources (for more on economic dependency, see below). Tactics include limiting access to income, denying access to bank accounts and financial information and imposing limits on the use of property.

- *Economic exploitation* is described as establishing an arrangement in which the victim's economic resources are used for the abuser's benefit, diminishing what the victim has built up and compromising their economic wellbeing – reversing the direction of dependence (see below for more on this). Tactics include 'freeloading' (demanding that the victim solely pay for household necessities, buy them goods or pay their bills); stealing the victim's money/property; or generating debt in the victim's name through fraud and/or coercion.

Qualitative research studies on economic abuse have also identified themes which are broadly consistent with the statistically tested constructs identified through the development of quantitative measurement scales.

Table Three. SEA-2 (Adams et al., 2019).

Economic restriction:

1. Decide how you could spend money rather than letting you spend it how you saw fit

2. Make you ask them for money

3. Keep financial information from you

4. Keep you from having the money you needed to buy food, clothing or other necessities

5. Hide money so that you could not find it

6. Demand that you give them receipts or change when you spent money

7. Keep you from having a job or going to work

Economic exploitation:

8. Spend their money however they wanted whilst your money went to pay for necessities

9. Make you use your money to buy them things or pay their bills when you didn't want to

10. Steal your property

11. Put bills in your name, leaving you to pay them

12. Force or pressure you to give them your savings or other assets

13. Make you take out a loan or buy something on credit when you didn't want to

14. Take out a loan or buy something on credit in your name without your permission

---

In the first piece of UK-based research on economic abuse, Sharp (2008) identified four types of economic control: interfering with education and employment (employment sabotage); controlling access to economic resources (economic restriction); refusing to contribute to household costs, making her work for him for free, trying to coerce her into prostitution (economic exploitation); and generating economic costs.[2]

The latter theme reflects behaviour through which the abuser creates additional costs which absorb available income, for example, disconnecting utilities and destroying a partner's belongings and/or household resources which then must then be reconnected/replaced (Anderson et al., 2003; Smallwood, 2015). Thus, despite the constructs being conceptually useful, they fail to capture all forms of economic control. Sharp-Jeffs (2021a) therefore suggests that the construct of employment sabotage (identified by Postmus et al., 2016) is expanded to economic sabotage, making the demonstrable impact on the ability of victim-survivors to maintain economic resources (see below) visible.

It follows then that Sharp-Jeffs (2021a) also suggests that the term 'any behaviour' within the economic abuse definition should be understood to include controlling tactics which sit under the constructs of economic restriction, exploitation and/or sabotage. In practice, and as illustrated within an analysis of successful prosecutions of the CCB offence (Sharp-Jeffs & Learmonth, 2017), abusers may use one or more of these strategies successively, simultaneously (see also Citizen's Advice, 2014; Sharp, 2008) or may switch between them all.

'Substantial Adverse Effect'

'Economic abuse' means any behaviour that has a substantial adverse effect *on B's ability to (a) acquire, use or maintain money or other property, or (b) obtain goods or services.*

The phrase 'substantial adverse effect' within the definition of economic abuse is also used in sub-clause 4b within section 76 of the Serious Crime Act (2015) which introduced the offence of CCB in intimate or familial relationships. For the CCB offence to apply, behaviour on the part of the perpetrator must take place 'repeatedly or continuously' and must have had a 'serious effect' on the victim, meaning that it has caused the victim to fear violence will be used against them on 'at least two occasions', or it has had a 'substantial adverse effect on the victims' day-to-day activities' (Home Office, 2015, p. 2).

76 Controlling or coercive behaviour in an intimate or family relationship

(1) A person (A) commits an offence if –

 (a) A repeatedly or continuously engages in behaviour towards another person (B) that is controlling or coercive,
 (b) at the time of the behaviour, A and B are personally connected,
 (c) the behaviour has a serious effect on B, and
 (d) A knows or ought to know that the behaviour will have a serious effect on B.

(2) A's behaviour has a 'serious effect' on B if – (a) it causes B to fear, on at least two occasions, that violence will be used against B, or (b) it causes B serious alarm or distress which has a substantial adverse effect on B's usual day-to-day activities.

The CCB offence recognises the harm caused by the cumulative impact of coercion or control on a victim-survivor, highlighting that 'a repeated pattern of abuse can be more injurious and harmful than a single incident of violence' (Home Office, 2015a, p. 3). This is articulated within the statutory definition of domestic abuse through reference to how abusive behaviour can be a 'course of conduct'.

ECONOMIC ABUSE WITHIN A COURSE OF CONDUCT

The idea of domestic abuse as a course of conduct is consistent with academic literature in which patterns or combinations of physical, sexual, emotional and economic abuse have been variously articulated (Kelly et al., 2014).

Again, as the Duluth Power and Control Wheel illustrates, alongside economic abuse, controlling tactics include isolation, intimidation, coercion and threats and the abuse of children. Physical and sexual violence are positioned within the rim of the wheel. This is significant since it illustrates how the coercive power derived from them is located not just in their actual use, but through ongoing intimidation – what *could* happen, based on previous experience (Kelly, 1988; Pence & Paymar, 1986). Coercive power is, therefore, predicated on the victim-survivor's belief that they can and will experience negative consequences for non-compliance (Dutton & Goodman, 2005). This creates a context in which refusing a demand is dangerous, compelling a victim-survivor to act in accordance with the abuser's wishes, rather than their own.

Similarly, Stark (2007, p. 272) uses the term 'coercive control' to explain how, as a structural form of deprivation, withholding money (and other necessities such as food) is interwoven with physical and sexual abuse, dictating choices and micro-regulating everyday actions. Degradation can be linked to deprivation but is also exercised through repeated acts and statements of disrespect which induce shame and self-blame, thus inhibiting disclosure. The victim-survivors' confidence in their capabilities and perceptions is undermined.

This is further enhanced via isolation which is designed to instil dependence and limits access to help or support, such that the abuser becomes the primary source of information and validation. Control is also exerted through intimidation which includes surveillance and degradation. Surveillance 'falls on a continuum of tactics' that ensure the victim-survivor knows that they are being watched (Kelly et al., 2014). In this way, coercive control is rarely confined to the home since it can extend into all the spaces that the victim-survivor enters, including their place of work. Furthermore, the exertion of coercive control is situationally specific – drawing on personalised knowledge of a victim-survivors' movements, habits, resources and vulnerabilities (Stark, 2007; see also Kelly et al., 2014).

Through this framing, Stark (2007) also illustrates how coercive control 'is ongoing rather than episodic' and 'that its effects are cumulative rather than incident-specific'. On this basis he argues that IPV is neither 'domestic' nor primarily about 'violence'. Indeed, he describes it, not as an assault crime, but a liberty crime in which a victim-survivors' freedom is limited by having to live within parameters set by the perpetrator. Whilst the impact of physical and sexual assault cannot and should not be underestimated, efforts to subvert a victim-survivors' right to autonomy prevent them from 'freely applying their agency in economic and political life' (Stark, 2007, p. 13).

The 'Technology' of Economic Abuse

> **CASE STUDY ONE:** Natalie's Story – Economic Abuse in the Context of Coercive Control.
>
> I met my ex through work and, at first, he seemed really nice and charming. He moved in with me at my parents' house six months after we met and proposed soon after. The first 18 months of our relationship were OK but, looking back, I realise that there were red flags from the beginning. For example, he constantly called me – 30 to 40 phone calls a day would not be unusual. If I didn't answer them all, he would become angry. Two weeks after we moved into our own flat, he turned aggressive. There were times of intimidation and bullying but it was not constant, it was every now and then. He would throw my phone across the room, damage my belongings; once he chucked my handbag out of the door and it went over the fence into the next-door neighbour's property. He would shout at me and bang items on work surfaces. He smashed up the kitchen. He started blaming everything on me. He'd say, 'I act like this because it's your fault'. Then these periods would pass, and he would attempt to appease me with gifts and promises. He would be full of apologies, buying me flowers and taking me for dinner. I thought I was going insane. I would experience severe panic and anxiety attacks.
>
> I did leave him, but he drew me back in with his pleas. He'd say, 'You're the best thing that ever happened to me, I can't get through this without you'. It was the guilt that kept me with him. I had started to completely neglect myself. It was so all-consuming. I was scared to leave the house. I cut myself off from

friends. When I tried to sleep, he would turn the stereo up loud. When I asked him to turn it down, he would put it on low and tell me I was imagining things. It was near constant psychological torture, and I was trying desperately every day to survive. As time went on, the abuse worsened. He'd scream and shout at me. He lost control in public. It would really embarrass me. He would push and shove me; not punches because they would be visible. On one occasion, I was resting in bed after an illness when he barged into the room and demanded money to go to the shops. As I logged into my banking app, he told me to hand over my phone and, within 10 minutes, he had applied for a £5,000 loan from my account. When the money came through, he transferred it to his own. Overall, his spending put me £80,000 in debt. He even quit his job. Years of fear meant that saying 'no' was not an option.

Then two things happened that made me realise I had to get out. Firstly, he chased me around our home with a knife. I thought I'd die trying to save myself. I thought I could avoid the worst physical, psychological and economic abuse if I did as I was told, but the thought of being stabbed took me to rock bottom. The second came when he marched me into a pawn shop to sell my wedding and engagement rings. Something clicked. I just thought, this is not love. I called a friend and asked her to pick me up. I arrived at my brother's house and told my family the full story. I went ahead with the prosecution because controlling and coercive behaviour – with its absence of physical violence – is still an abstract concept to some. I want to share my experience so others might recognise they are victims too.[3][4][5][6]

ECONOMIC ABUSE AND ITS LINKS TO OTHER FORMS OF CONTROL

Reflecting Natalie's experience, research has uncovered statistical correlations between economic abuse and physical and psychological abuse, as well as tactics such as isolation. Adams et al. (2008) undertook research with female survivors of IPV and found that higher levels of economic abuse were significantly related to higher levels of physical and psychological abuse. A longitudinal study examining the impact of a financial literacy programme with survivors of IPV undertaken by Postmus, Plummer, McMahon, Shaanta Murshid, and Sung Kim (2012b) found that participants who experienced physical and psychological abuses more frequently were also subject to more monitoring and restrictions related to their use of financial resources (see also Postmus et al., 2016). In addition, Weaver, Sanders, Campbell, & Schnabel (2009) uncovered data which suggested that economic abuse is particularly associated with the experience of emotional/verbal abuse and isolation for female victims of IPV living in US domestic violence shelters.

The strong correlation between economic abuse and psychological/emotional abuse is perhaps unsurprising since economic abuse has previously been conceptualised as a form of psychological abuse (Loring, 1994). Sharp (2008) powerfully illustrates this through the Economic Power and Control Wheel. This adapts the Duluth Power and Control Wheel to articulate how economic abuse overlaps with, threads through and reinforces other forms of coercive control.

For instance, behaviours linked to economic abuse can also give rise to emotional abuse. These include constantly telling her she is worthless, whilst making her feel worthless – making her account for every penny because she cannot be trusted to manage money; or denying her access to necessities

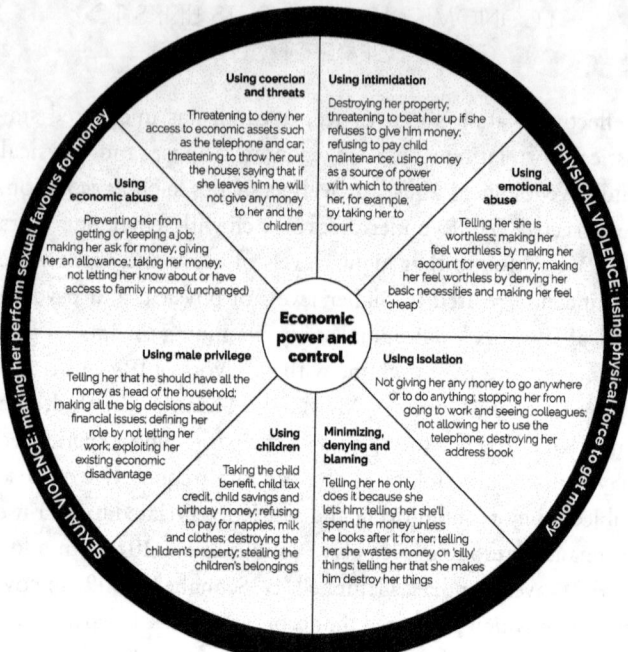

Figure Two. The Economic Power and Control Wheel (Sharp, 2008).

Source: Adapted with permission from Domestic Abuse Intervention, 202 East Superior Street, Duluth, Minnesota 55802, 218-722-2781. www.theduluthmodel.org

such as food, water, heat, clothing and toiletries. Similarly, isolation can be created by not giving her any money to go anywhere or do anything; stopping her from going to work and seeing her colleagues; and not allowing her to use the car, telephone, etc. This is explored further within Chapter Two's discussion on the impact of economic abuse.

When economic abuse is experienced in this way, victim-survivors also describe it as being 'constant' and 'ongoing' (see also Robinson, 2003) which saps the victim-survivors energy and also makes it difficult to find a moment of autonomy within which to seek help (Stark, 2007).

> *It was constant abuse the economic abuse – but you don't feel it, you don't hurt from it – it was ongoing which most probably kept me down more than a smack. (Sharp, 2008)*

Paradoxically, Sharp (2008) suggests that this might be another reason why economic abuse is not always recognised by victim-survivors. Unsurprisingly, very few victim-survivors describe experiencing economic abuse in isolation (Sharp-Jeffs, 2015a).

ECONOMIC ABUSE AS A 'SINGLE INCIDENT'

The Explanatory Notes to the Domestic Abuse Act (2021) state that the purpose of including the qualification 'substantial and adverse effect' within the definition of economic abuse is to ensure that isolated incidents, such as damaging someone's car, or not disclosing financial information, are not inadvertently captured. At the same time, however, this is inconsistent with 'abusive' behaviour at clause 1 within the statutory definition of domestic abuse which sets out that 'it does not matter whether the behaviour consists of a single incident or a course of conduct'.

Prior to the CCB offence coming into force, common criminal offences linked to domestic abuse included single incidents of economic abuse – including, for example, criminal damage. This has remained consistent. In the 2017 analysis of successful prosecutions undertaken by SEA, just eight cases involved the charge of CCB alone. In addition to grievous bodily harm, actual bodily harm and assault, other criminal offences charged included: criminal damage, theft, arson and animal cruelty. This is also noted within a Home Office review of the CCB offence suggesting that, even where CCB has been recognised and recorded, investigating this offence may not be prioritised due to the difficulty in collecting evidence (Home Office, 2021). Qualitative research by Wiener (2017) identified challenges that the police face in taking statements related to coercive control when they are not 'an event':

> *So, if it's an assault, or a criminal damage [case], there's an event. Whereas obviously with coercive control you are telling a narrative, a story – that's always going to be much more difficult. (Focus group police participant, Wiener, 2017, p. 505)*

Sharp-Jeffs (2021a) therefore argues that attention needs to be given to the suggestion that single incidents of economic abuse would not fall under this definition. This is also important, if as Kelly and Westmarland (2014) claim, AFV usually consists of single incidents.

ECONOMIC ABUSE IN THE CONTEXT OF AFV

The intention of recognising family members within the 2005 policy definition of domestic violence was to recognise the gendered crimes of Female Genital Mutilation (FGM), so-called 'honour' based violence (HBV) and forced marriage. Some 'by and for' women's organisations welcomed this development and saw it as progressive to bring forms of violence experienced by black and minoritised women and girls into the mainstream. However, Kelly and Westmarland (2014) describe it as a 'hindrance' rather than as a help. They argue that because family violence usually consists of single incidents, insertion of the new 'any incident' wording within the policy definition served not only to obscure the reality of IPV but assumed that the dynamics are the same when they are not (Kelly & Westmarland, 2014).

This disconnect has been recognised in the research literature. An analysis of 32 domestic homicide cases, for example, highlighted that, because the commonly used domestic abuse, stalking and honour-based violence (DASH) risk identification tool was developed from research on IPV, some risk factors were simply not relevant in relation to the family violence cases. In fact, just one of the eight family homicide cases was risk assessed, compared to eight of the twenty-four intimate partner homicide cases which may suggest that agencies do not consider the DASH appropriate in family cases where the victim-survivor is over 16 years of age. Certainly, a report by Her Majesty's Inspectorate of Constabulary (HMIC, 2014) noted that some forces have developed a policy of not completing the full DASH form in certain circumstances, including cases of AFV.

Since the new statutory definition of domestic abuse also recognises family members this is highly relevant. Sharp-Jeffs and Kelly (2016) suggest a revised tool is probably needed for adult family cases, one which will need to be developed as more knowledge accrues. A brief review of the literature on commons forms of AFV (see below) reveals that it is almost certainly the case that power derived from economic resources is used across a range of different forms of family violence.

PARENT TO ADOLESCENT/ADULT ABUSE

Forced Marriage

Anitha and Gill (2009, p. 180) state that, within legal and policy discourse, arranged marriage and forced marriage continue to be framed in binary terms and the context in which consent is constructed largely remains unexplored. They argue that consent and coercion in relation to marriage can be better understood as two ends of a continuum, between which lie 'degrees of socio-cultural expectation, control, persuasion, pressure, threat and force in the context of gendered inequalities'.

An examination of case law on forced marriage reveals that existing conceptualisations of coercion now take into consideration emotional pressure as well as the role of physical force (Anitha & Gill, 2009). It is interesting to note that the emotional pressures cited as grounds for duress within the case of *Hirani v. Hirani* were that the victim-survivor was financially dependent on her parents and that they had threatened to turn her out of the home if she did not go through with the marriage. In this case, economic abuse is again subsumed within the category of emotional abuse, despite feminists having long recognised that the structural constraints that give rise to 'coercive potential' include poverty. Financial abuse is, however, recognised as a form of duress within multi-agency statutory guidance on forced marriage, along with physical, psychological, sexual and emotional pressure (HM Government, 2014).

Research by Samad and Eade (2002) and Sharp-Jeffs (2016b) further suggests that South Asian women actively assess the emotional, financial, physical and cultural cost of saying 'yes' or 'no' to marriage proposals in a situation of inequality. Family members may also seek to redress power imbalances such as financial control through confiscation of wages/income as a means of exit. For instance, in describing the murder of Shafilea Ahmed, Gill (2014) shares how her ambition had been to go to university and to become a barrister. She got a part-time job and had saved up more than £1,000 before her parents stole her money by forcing her to withdraw her savings. On the night of her murder, money was found in her handbag.

So-called HBV

Additional risks for victim-survivors of so-called HBV outlined in a report by SafeLives (2017, p. 8) include 'common difficulties relating to housing and finance'. It is noted that, in some instances of HBV, the victim and perpetrator may have jointly owned a home for a long time. This can be challenging, making it harder for the victim to move away, especially if s/he has long-term support networks nearby (see Chapter Four). Financial issues are recognised to exacerbate this situation if the victim has never been financially independent. Perpetrators of HBV often include partners and family members, both of whom may control finances as part of the abuse.

It is further acknowledged that financial and benefit issues also relate to immigration status, which in some cases will be unresolved or dependent on the perpetrator (see Chapter Two). In addition, some victims-survivors will be sharing living space with other families which may contravene tenancy regulations, thereby acting as a barrier to seeking help since doing so, will require reaching out to someone in an official capacity (SafeLives, 2017) and potentially becoming homeless. Research indicates that the 'anti-immigration' agenda results in many women from black and minoritised communities being less likely to access statutory services for help. This is because their experience of violence at home cannot be separated from wider structures of racism (Anitha & Gill, 2009). Non-disclosure arises from women's desire to avoid reinforcing essentialist stereotypes of them and their communities (Rai & Thiara, 1997) leading Wilson (2010) to argue that their location at the intersection of multiple dominatory systems creates numerous contradictions, including jeopardising the ability to challenge violence (see also Balzani, 2010).

Female Genital Mutilation

If FGM also occurs within a context of coercion and control, then multi-agency statutory guidance pays little attention to this. Legal guidance on FGM for the Crown Prosecution Service (CPS, 2019) does however recognise evidence of a financial benefit or incentive to the offence when building a case.[7] For example, women cutters may rely on this work for an income and their own financial independence and so this may lead them to collude in duress (SEA, 2021b).

ADOLESCENT/ADULT-TO-PARENT VIOLENCE AND ABUSE (APVA)

Hunter and Nixon (2012, p. 211) describe the issue of adolescent/adult child-to-parent abuse as 'one of the most unacknowledged and under-researched forms of family violence'. The CSEW does not routinely measure child-to-parent violence, last doing so in the mid-1990s when the British Crime Survey found that this form of violence reflected around 3% of domestic violence cases (Mirrlees-Black, Mayhew, & Percy, 1996). International studies spanning more than four decades have, however, consistently concluded that this form of abuse is highly gendered, with the majority of population, community, criminal justice and clinical/service studies finding that mothers are significantly more likely than fathers to experience abuse from their children (Simmons, McEwan, Purcell, & Ogloff, 2018; Westmarland, 2015).

A Home Office information guide states that it is important to recognise that APVA is likely to involve a pattern of behaviour which can include different types of abusive behaviours, including physical violence as well as damage to property, emotional abuse and economic/financial abuse

(Home Office, 2015b). This is also a theme identified within a recent rapid review of APVA undertaken by Baker and Bonnick (2021) for the Domestic Abuse Commissioner's Office. The researchers summarise evidence which recognises that it can involve the destruction of property, including damage to the family home. Accounts from parents also include examples such as the theft or destruction of the family car, demanding or stealing money, punching holes in walls and kicking through doors, destroying personal items and the tearing or theft of clothes. As is the case for intimate partners, this can have significant financial implications for parents through having to pay for repairs or replacements, as well as in some cases, being evicted from their homes.

The Home Office guide goes on to cite from Groves and Thomas' (2014) findings that again, as is also the case for IPV, APVA appears to affect all levels of society. Although many parents reporting this form of violence to the police are not in full-time employment and some are struggling with financial and housing problems; others are in professional jobs earning high incomes.

ELDER ABUSE

Financial abuse is one of the most prevalent forms of elder abuse. Research suggests that financial exclusion, low levels of financial capability and cognitive impairment can mean that older people become dependent upon others to manage their finances or to access their income or savings. This reliance on others for assistance, including family members, can easily be abused (Crosby, Clark, Hayes, Jones, & Lievesley, 2008). As Chapter Two will discuss, it is important not to assume elder abuse when financial abuse arises in the context of a partner taking on a caring role for their partner since this may be a sign of ongoing coercive control (Sharp-Jeffs & Kelly, 2016).

Fitzgerald (2004) reports that men are slightly more likely to experience financial abuse than women (23% men; 21% women) but suggests that, overall, more women than men are identified as experiencing elder abuse because they live longer than men and are consequently more likely to be living alone. It is noted that an issue arising for owner-occupiers may include pressures concerning inheritance of the family home (Rowlingson, 2006). Anecdotal evidence in an affluent London Borough draws parallels between the taking over of the homes of drug users/vulnerable young people by criminal gangs – referred to as cuckooing – and a similar practice by adult children taking over the homes of their vulnerable parents as they are unable to afford to live in the area.

As Chapter Two will illustrate, there are advantages to adopting a structural lens to analysing these issues since approaches to AFV have tended to ignore factors such as gender and have instead constructed such abuse as an individual, medical, behavioural or criminal issue (Wilcox, 2012).

'Acquire, Use or Maintain'

> *'Economic abuse'* means any behaviour that has a substantial adverse effect on B's ability to (a) acquire, use or maintain *money or other property*, or (b) obtain goods or services.

The definition of economic abuse within the Domestic Act (2021) clearly draws on the academic definition developed by Adams et al. (2008).

The 'Technology' of Economic Abuse

Economic abuse involves behaviours that control a person's ability to acquire, use, or maintain economic resources, thus threatening their economic security and potential for self-sufficiency. (p. 564)

The controlling behaviours (economic restriction, exploitation and sabotage) explored above prevent resource acquisition, resource use and resource maintenance. SEA's analysis of successful CCB prosecutions used the categories of acquire, use and maintain to organise examples of economic abuse. As such, the examples in Table Four reflect the real-life experiences of victim-survivors.

Table Four. Examples of Preventing Resource Acquisition, Use and Maintenance (Sharp & Learmonth, 2017).

Resource acquisition:

- Made her leave her job; threatened to get her sacked; pressured her into reducing her working hours.

Resource use:

- Kept all but £500 of her monthly wages of £2,000; gave her an allowance of £10 per week after taking all her bank cards
- Restricted access to her bank account
- Monitored her bank transactions
- Checked her receipts
- Confiscated her phone; cancelled her mobile phone contract
- Refused to put credit on the gas or electric metre
- Took the keys to her car; used her car, leaving her to catch the bus/walk to work

Resource maintenance:

- Smashed her mobile phone
- Burned her clothes/threw away her clothes

Table Four   (Continued)

- Demanded she 'lent' him money and did not pay her back (in one case £5,000)
- Threatened to smash up her home; threatened to pour paint over the carpets and her belongings; threatened to burn her house down (including with the victim in it)
- Took her bank and credit cards and emptied the joint bank account
- Demanded the money from her bank account
- Demanded she take a £50,000 debt for him
- Refused to leave the house she was paying rent for
- Damaged or threatened to damage her parent's property

In a critical assessment of the economic abuse definition, Sharp-Jeffs (2021a) observes that it is unclear why sub-section (b) was introduced setting out the victim-survivors' ability to 'obtain' goods and services, since to obtain an economic resource could be interpreted in the same way as 'acquiring' it (as set out in a).

Moreover, and as the examples above have shown, perpetrators can prevent victim-survivors from using or maintaining goods and services in the same way they do money or other property – for instance, stopping a partner from using the car or disconnecting utilities. For this reason, Sharp-Jeffs (2021a) suggests that sub-sections (a) and (b) of clause 1(4) should be merged in practice so that there is recognition that perpetrators may also prevent a partner from using or maintaining goods or services.

ECONOMIC DEPENDENCY AND INSECURITY

Understanding how abusers prevent their partner/family member from acquiring, using and maintaining economic resources is valuable in illustrating how economic abuse can happen to anyone. Abusers take advantage of existing economic inequality and dependency. For this reason, women are more likely to experience economic abuse (see Chapter Two). But, at the same time, abusers will seek to destroy a partner's existing economic independence by creating the conditions for dependence and/or by creating economic insecurity. As Adams et al. (2019) suggest, an abuser may 'forcibly' create a situation in which a victim-survivor is economically dependent on them. A victim-survivor may be prevented from going to work and acquiring an independent income. Alternatively, they may be allowed to work, but prevented from accessing their income, for example, by being denied a debit card to their bank account. This prevents them from using a resource they already have.

> **CASE STUDY TWO:** Amy's Story – Creating Economic Dependency.
>
> I had a law degree and was general counsel at a multinational software firm before I was forced to give up work. After I gave up my career, I became increasingly isolated. His control increased and worsened. Without my own income, I found myself suddenly financially dependent. I had very limited access to money and would have to have a specific need for it if he was to grant me any. When I'd worked, we were earning a combined figure of almost £200,000 a year, but he drained every single penny out of our joint account over the next few years. He told me he didn't feel we could afford anything. He would not let me see or discuss his finances.

> When I ran away, he deliberately kept me under siege for years, by taking me back and back to court. The divorce drained me of every single penny. He also refused to pay any child maintenance. At one point we were down to living off one egg each a day. It took years for me to accept that there was sexual abuse, it was just so distressing, the physical abuse, the strangling, the beatings. But that was minor compared to the emotional and economic abuse.
>
> I am hypervigilant and find it hard to trust people, so I have not met anyone new. I have low self-confidence. All this means that 6 years after the divorce I am still only about 80 per cent of the person I was before I met him. I am too old to be considered relevant to my previous career which has meant a tough start at the bottom of the career ladder in another job. I am not a stupid woman; this could happen to anybody.

Dependency via economic restriction tends to be assumed in cases of economic abuse. But economic abuse cases do not always follow this pattern. Instead, the victim-survivors' economic resources may be used for the abuser's benefit. Adams et al. (2019) describe this within the context of economic exploitation – diminishing the economic resources that the victim-survivor has built up and compromising their economic wellbeing.

Adams et al. (2019) give examples of economic exploitation – for example, freeloading (refusing to contribute, Sharp, 2008), stealing money/property and coerced debt. Yet, as Sharp-Jeffs (2021a) argues, economic sabotage is another strategy which prevents a victim-survivor from maintaining economic resources through having to replace expensive and much-needed items such as mobile phones or laptops. Thomas (2018, p. 119) writes how sabotage leaves a victim-survivor feeling like there is never 'quite enough' spare money and stops them from creating any 'financial traction'.

The assertion that economic exploitation reverses 'the direction of dependence' needs to be questioned. The research literature and practice examples (see Case Study Three) give examples of abusers using this tactic in a way that enables them to simultaneously maintain and grow their own economic resources (Sharp-Jeffs, 2021a).

> **CASE STUDY THREE:** Annie's Story – Creating Economic Insecurity.
>
> When I had my first baby, just before I turned 29, I had been married for eight years, managed 19 staff, and earned more than my husband. He could be rude and aggressive in company, but I always stuck up for him at the cost of becoming estranged from my own family.
>
> When the baby was born the balance of power shifted – I was made redundant while on maternity leave and he got a pay rise and promotion. I took a lower-paid, part-time job but he refused to share the cost of childcare or increase the amount he paid towards household expenses. He had always paid the mortgage on our home, with me responsible for everything else. But when two more children followed within four years, I struggled to cover food, bills, clothes, shoes, and other essentials.
>
> He also began paying his credit card bills, for luxury items and holidays for himself, from the household

accounts. So, we had his account, my account, and a joint bills account. He would buy himself stuff on the credit cards, and the more he spent the more the direct debit increased, and I would have to put more money in. The result was that he had tons of money because his spending, on items like motorbikes, high-end photographic equipment, and designer clothes, was all charged to the joint account. Meanwhile I would get up every Sunday morning and buggy the kids around a boot sale to buy them 20p trousers.

My ex became increasingly violent – by the end of our marriage he was beating me daily. He started hitting me after the birth of our first baby. He was completely remorseful after he'd done it the first time and I had flowers and he was crying and said he would never do it again. It's not like someone comes into your life one day and they hit you. They work on you slowly at first so you will put up with being hit ... I was so isolated ... you're so controlled by that point.

I went full-time at work in a bid to bring in more money, but I still didn't have enough to pay for his lifestyle or for the food for all of us, so I got an evening cleaning job. For five years I worked 60 hours a week, sleeping only four or five hours a night. After a full day at work, I would put the children to bed and go to my cleaning job at 21:00, finishing there at 01:00 and getting up again at 06:00 as he didn't like the youngsters waking him. Not only that, but he would also insist on dinner, just for himself, all paid for and cooked by me, ready on a tray when he came in from work every night. Failure would result in a beating.

He blamed me for our financial problems, accusing me of being unable to manage my money. I felt guilty even replacing a pair of broken shoes. The bank encouraged me to take out a loan to pay off a £7,500 overdraft on the joint account, but they failed to close the overdraft, so he ran it up again. I took out another loan and this time the bank did cancel the overdraft. But with no overdraft, his spending quickly emptied the joint account, so the bank turned to my account and, emptied this too. It finally drew funds from his account, and we met one lunchtime in the town centre to discuss it. He swung a punch at my face and as I ran off to go back to work, he said: 'You can run but I am going to finish the job when I get home'.

At work, I broke down in a meeting and my boss took me aside and handed me the number of a women's refuge. I just picked the kids up from school and we drove – and that was it. I stayed in the refuge for six weeks before returning home once he'd been persuaded to leave. I had to get an injunction and a panic alarm to stop him coming to the house, screaming abuse and attacking friends. But, even with the loss of his income, we were instantly better off once he had gone.

Overall, once all the credit cards, store cards and direct debits had come in, I was left with debts of about £58,000. I also took over the mortgage, determined to keep our home. The bank tried to repossess the house, but I won on appeal, and they wrote off £8,000 of what I owed. I finally cleared the debt – 12 years after the marriage ended – and have almost paid off the mortgage. The house is shabby and bare but at least it is mine.[8]

Not only does the refusal to contribute to household expenses drain a women's economic resources, but it means that individuals within the same household may have 'radically different standards of living' (Littwin, 2012, p. 984; see also Thomas, 2018) like Annie. This results in what Branigan (2004, p. ii) describes as a 'feminisation of poverty within relationships'.

Furthermore, it is common for an abuser to manipulate a family's financial assets and debts so that all the assets (such as deeds to houses, or titles of cars) are in their name and all the debts in their partner's name (Citizen's Advice, 2014; Howard & Skipp, 2015; Littwin, 2012; Lyon, 2002). Thomas (2018, p. 137) describes this as 'an asset structure that solely benefits the abuser' and can be years in the making.

'SCHEMERS'

Cameron's (2014) typology of financially abusive perpetrators recognises that there may be extreme cases where individuals enter a relationship with the primary objective of taking the other parties' money and financial assets (schemers). Anecdotal evidence arising from domestic homicide reviews (DHRs) suggests that this does take place, usually when the abuser is younger than the victim-survivor. The abuser may describe themselves as a 'carer' to the outside world but lead the victim-survivor to believe they are in intimate relationship with them (see Sharp-Jeffs & Kelly, 2016).

Predatory Marriage

Closely linked to this, and the discussion on elder abuse above, is 'predatory marriage' – a term which originated in

Canada, where several provinces have altered their laws to insert safeguards aimed at protecting vulnerable people from being coerced into unions to which they do not have the capacity to consent.[9]

CASE STUDY FOUR: Jean's Story – Written by Her Daughter (Predatory Marriage).

My mother was a widow of eighty-seven when she met the man. She said she met him by the garden gate, but we're not sure whether that is true as she already had a diagnosis of vascular dementia.

We lived next door to her and saw her several times a day. The first we knew of the man was that his possessions were suddenly in her house. She often asked what his name was, where he came from, and where he lived. 'Did you get him for me?' she'd ask. The man called himself 'her carer' and nobody in authority seemed to question that. We were told 'He's there at your mother's invitation'. I tried to explain that she did not know he lived there, with no success.

Initially the man was very over-friendly to us and plied my mother with cards and flowers. As time went on, he became colder and colder to us and took to keeping the door locked from the inside. He told everyone that I did not love my mother, even though we lived next door, always went on holiday together, and had belonged to the same drama group for many years. I felt crushed and powerless. We asked my mother's GP, social services, the police, and a solicitor for help but nobody seemed able to do anything – sometimes we were met by disbelief and dismissal.

> The family solicitor reassured us that my mother would not be able to make a new will or to marry because of her dementia. Yet two days after her death in March 2016 the man arrived at her GP surgery with a marriage certificate. He had married her in total secrecy five months before her death. My mother was in her early-nineties, and he was in his mid-sixties. The witnesses were the man's son and a lady from the pub. My mother never had any idea that they were married.
>
> The Police tried to prosecute the man for forced marriage, but the CPS said that they could not prosecute him because no evidence – no audio or video recordings – is kept at marriage, even though one of the registrars had raised the issue of my mother's capacity on the day of the wedding because my mother could not answer some of the questions. I had registered Power of Attorney but there is no link with marriage so there was no requirement to tell me that the man was planning to marry my mother.
>
> My mother had made a will, but the marriage revoked that. This man inherited her whole estate, including all the possessions in her house. It also gave him total control over her funeral. My mother is buried in an unmarked grave and we are not allowed to put up a headstone because the man owns the grave plot. The man remarried soon after.
>
> The impact on our family has been devastating, both emotionally and financially.'

Romance Fraud

'Romance frauds' are another example of a situation in which an individual believes they are in a relationship with someone who is 'scheming' to gain financially. This form of economic abuse tends to take place online, for example, via dating websites. The victim-survivor is groomed into believing they are in a relationship and asked to send money to the abuser. According to UK Finance, there was a 20% increase in bank transfer fraud linked to romance scams between 2019 and 2020.[10]

'Money, Other Property, Goods and Services'

> *'Economic abuse' means any behaviour that has a substantial adverse effect on B's ability to (a) acquire, use or maintain money or other property, or (b) obtain goods or services.*

In line with the argument put forward by Littwin (2012), the wording of the economic abuse definition within the Act reflects a broader understanding of financial abuse, by referring not only to money, but also 'other property' and 'goods or services'.

Commentary on the provisions found in the Explanatory Notes to the Act further expand on these terms:

> *'Property' would cover items such a mobile phone or a car and, also include pets or other animals (for example agricultural livestock).*

> *'Goods and services' would cover, for example, utilities such as heating, or items such as food and clothing.*

Adams et al. (2019) developed the term 'targets of control' to describe the wide range of economic resources which perpetrators seek to interfere with. Table Five gives examples, including those recognised within the Explanatory Notes to the Act.

Table Five. Targets of Control.

Money or Other Property	Goods and Services
Employment and earned income (wages)	Utilities such as heating, water, internet
Other income/money – family income, benefit payments, inheritances and monetary gifts, pension payments	Banking services
Mobile phone	Credit services
Pets or other animals	Food
Housing	Clothing
Transportation (car, train/bus pass)	
Employment	
Laptops, tablets, etc.	
Necessities such as toiletries	

ADDRESSING 'ONGOING' ECONOMIC ABUSE WITHIN THE DOMESTIC ABUSE ACT (2021)

In a roundtable discussion on economic abuse facilitated for the Home Office/Ministry of Justice, victim-survivors explained that, after leaving the abuser the economic control they experienced did not end. They described dealing with ongoing repercussions arising from the economic control exerted by the abuser when living/in a relationship with him. For many, this was whilst simultaneously experiencing economic abuse post-separation (SEA, 2018).

This meant that they were faced with the challenge of 'rebuilding back' before they could move forward, yet in the context of ongoing interference. One woman described this situation as 'relentless' and another testified that it could continue for decades. According to SEA and the charity Advocacy After Fatal Domestic Abuse (AAFDA), economic control can even continue after a victim-survivor dies – whether by suicide or homicide.

Ongoing Repercussions of Economic Abuse

Since economic abuse is designed to reinforce/create economic dependence and/or insecurity, an immediate impact of leaving an abuser is that victim-survivors lack the resources required for day-to-day survival (Adams et al., 2008; Smallwood, 2015). Many women leave with nothing and must start again from scratch. They may be homeless or forced to relocate hundreds of miles away due to a combination of safety reasons and access to refuge accommodation (Coy, Kelly, Foord, & Bowstead, 2011; Walby & Allen, 2004). They may be unable to use bank accounts or credit cards if there is the possibility that their new location might show up on financial statements going to their former address (Bell & Kober, 2008). Women who do access refuge accommodation may have to give up their job – again, due to a combination of safety reasons, the distance they must flee and/or because of the high rent which includes both accommodation and support costs (Liberal Democrats, 2009; Women's National Commission, 2003). Without a source of income, or perhaps even a bank account to pay money into, they may struggle to access welfare benefits or sources of credit.

As illustrated by the SEA-scales developed by Adams et al. (2008, 2019) and Postmus et al. (2016) keeping financial information from a partner is a common form of economic abuse. This means that the full extent of the abuse may take some time to discover and unravel. For example, they may be confronted with unknown debts in their name after leaving (Barron, 2012; Glinski, 2021).

Relevant measures called for as the Domestic Abuse Act progressed through parliament included emergency financial support for victim-survivors of domestic abuse (The Children's Society, 2020) and a period of paid employment leave (VAWG Sector, 2021).

Economic Abuse Post-separation

It is common for coercive control to continue after a victim-survivor has left (Tuerkheimer, 2013) and this is particularly the case for economic abuse since it does not require physical proximity to perpetrate (Stark, 2007). This means that it may continue, escalate or even start post-separation (Bell & Kober, 2008; Branigan, 2004; Camilleri, Corrie, & Moore, 2015; Citizen's Advice, 2014; Howard & Skipp, 2015; Kelly et al., 2014; Sharp, 2008; Smallwood, 2015; Wilcox, 2006). Again, Westmarland (2015, p. 42) observed that 'the financial abuses perpetrated against a woman by a violent partner seem consistent in many ways with the crime of harassment and this is even more the case once a relationship has ended'.

Kelly et al. (2014) found that ongoing control of women's economic resources was a direct interference by the perpetrator in their efforts to increase their space for action after leaving. Although some of the tactics used post-separation will be a continuation of those used by the perpetrator when the victim was in a relationship/living with them, research has shown that abusers will seek out new targets for control, adopting behaviours that are particular to the post-separation context (Sharp-Jeffs, 2015a).

A Cooperative Bank/Refuge survey found that behaviours that remain the same include damaging/stealing property, spending money from the joint account, spending money in their partner's personal account, running up bills in their partner's name and interfering with employment (Sharp-Jeffs, 2015b; see also Kelly et al., 2014). New behaviours include refusing to give child support/maintenance, prolonging the sale of joint property and taking their partner to court, resulting in financial costs. Indeed, the paper accompanying the publication of the draft Domestic Abuse Bill acknowledged the criminal and family court systems as mechanisms used by perpetrators to generate legal costs for a victim-survivor (HM Government, 2019).

> **CASE STUDY FIVE:** Layla's Story – Economic Abuse Post-separation.
>
> 'Me and my ex-husband jointly owned the home we lived in. He was controlling throughout the marriage. He would frequently pressurise me to transfer money into his bank account and he'd force me to let him use my credit card and take out bank loans. Rather than paying down the mortgage throughout our marriage he continuously borrowed on it without my consent.
>
> A week before he left for good, he made me sign over a substantial amount of equity in our home – I didn't know it at the time, but he wanted to fund his new life. I'd been invited to join a Christmas work do for his team at a hotel. I went to the room we were staying in and knocked on the door. He opened it, shut it behind me and took me over to a table with some paperwork on it. He sat on a chair and gestured that I sit on the bed. Almost immediately he launched into a speech about wanting £100,000 urgently. He didn't tell me why and when I asked, he said: 'You don't need to

know that' as he always did. I said I did, and it wasn't fair over and over again, but he still refused to tell me – he just kept shouting at me to sign. I was crying and he told me to be quiet, that everyone would hear and that I should get on with it.

I knew from all the previous experiences when he had intimidated me how this was going to go. He would pull and push me around, chase after me grabbing me, yanking me, and squeezing me forcibly and attempting to break down doors to get to me, so I knew that I couldn't get away – that I had no choice. I knew his strength and I knew he would stop at nothing until I signed. He had been shouting at me for nearly 25 years and I always had to do what he wanted. We were high up in the hotel, I had my back to the door and the door was locked, I had no means of escape and nowhere to go. When I did sign, he suddenly snapped back into happy mode. The money was transferred a few days later and he left after Christmas.

After my ex-husband left, he stopped contributing towards mortgage payments and household bills. Three months later, he arrived at the house and took me into the lounge saying he needed to take another £30,000 out of the mortgage and that he would pay it back. I protested and he became very aggressive, forcing me down onto a sofa whilst he screamed in my face. I was crying hysterically. When one of the children came into the room, also crying and asking what the matter was I stopped the ordeal to protect them and signed. By the end of that year, using similar methods, he had managed to secure a further £20,000 out of the mortgage account, it was at that point that the bank froze the account.

> He continues to use my contact details rather than his own. I am regularly chased by creditors for money and visited by bailiffs demanding payment of debts in my name of which I had no prior knowledge. I'm having to continuously pay off his debts and we're experiencing real hardship. I was unable to afford legal representation during the divorce proceedings and had to face his legal team as a litigant in person. The family court did not take any of his conduct (which included economic, emotional and sexual abuse) into consideration and although I have been left to bring up the children with no financial support, the judge gave an order for me to sell the house so that he could have 50 percent of the remaining equity. I have also had to pay him out of my business. The police won't do anything because all this happened before the change on the law. I now have 30 years' worth of evidence and I am still battling to get justice.

Many of these behaviours are described within the 'Post-Separation Economic Power and Control' Wheel developed by Glinski (2021) (Figure Three). Again, an adaptation of the original Duluth Power and Control Wheel, it represents what she calls the 'second' and 'third' stages of economic abuse: the consequences (or repercussions) of economic abuse arising from economic abuse experienced when in a relationship with the abuser (inner rim); and post-separation abuse (within the eight spokes).

The outermost rim highlights how, despite being physically separated, victim-survivors still fear their (ex)partners and the unpredictability of their abusive behaviour. The continuous

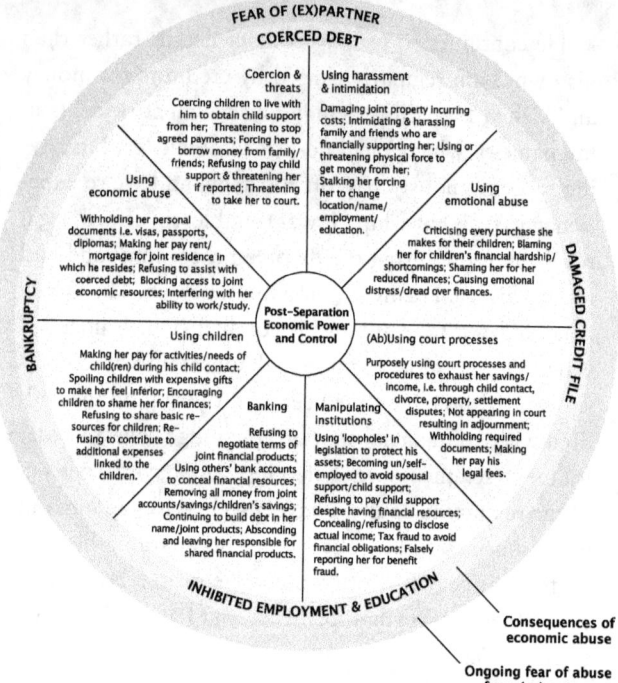

Figure Three. Post-separation Economic Power and Control (Glinski, 2021).

Source: Adaption of the original Power and Control Wheel approved by The Domestic Abuse Intervention Programmes.

fear that women live with post-separation (see also Kelly et al., 2014) therefore holds the wheel together.

Economic Abuse After Fatal Domestic Abuse

SEA and AAFDA have drawn attention to cases of suicide/ homicide where they are aware of an abuser benefitting from life insurance payouts and/or disposing of, and even selling, the victim's economic assets. Abusers can continue to control joint assets, including after prosecution for murder/manslaughter, for example, via frustrating the sale of a property (Orr, 2020), thereby withholding vital funds. A study on domestic homicide found that 11 children were living with family members who were struggling financially (Stanley, Chantler, & Robbins, 2019).

> **CASE STUDY SIX:** Emily's Story – Told by Her Dad (Economic Control After Fatal Domestic Abuse).
>
> One day, some years ago, we were suddenly contacted by our daughter's ex-husband. She had become an alcoholic and he was effectively throwing her out of the family home. His motive was to protect the children, but there were no explanations as to the underlying issues which drove Emily to insulate herself by drinking.
>
> What was slowly revealed when she opened-up to us was that she had been coercively controlled. I attended numerous meetings with Emily through her separation and divorce process, with lawyers, but also social services, the police, and other agencies. On reflection not one of them supported her. The ex-husband always managed to get in ahead of those meetings and gaslighted the professionals – they seemed to have no idea what he was doing to them. Emily was always on the back foot, despite people being presented with the 'truth' by myself.
>
> The process through which she went to get a financial settlement facilitated ongoing economic abuse.

He kept taking her back to the family court. She was not eligible for legal aid (see Chapter Five) and so had to take out a loan against the potential equity share in the ex-family home – the home that her ex-husband 'avoided' selling, thereby racking up more interest whilst Emily was alive. The liability grew to over £100,000.

Emily always said, 'she did not know she could leave'. In effect she never could because even the divorce settlement effectively legalised his control. Ultimately, the alcohol caught up with her and she died.

Emily had some credit card debts. When the bank contacted my wife and I they assumed, as next-of-kin, we would be the Administrators. But because our daughter died without a valid will, her ex-husband was able to become an Administrator for her estate – the ultimate irony. Once again, against the background of a legal mechanism, Emily's divorced ex-husband had been granted power over her assets. We ourselves are still suffering from his controlling behaviour, as we try to rebuild our lives. We have not seen our grandchildren since our daughter's funeral.

Coercive control remains a hidden form of abuse even to professionals and lawyers. The impact is not just on the abused but on their wider family and friends. Some elements of the divorce process and existing law can re-enforce the ability of abusers to continue to control, even after the abused has passed away. Some lessons are being learnt but there is still so much more change required, whether legally, financially, behaviourally, or educationally.

Rest in peace Emily – you are finally free.

INSTITUTIONAL ECONOMIC ABUSE

As the case study above illustrates, much of this behaviour is facilitated through the manipulation and use of policies, procedures and processes. Sharp (2008) calls this 'institutional economic abuse' and it can take place across different realms, including statutory and financial services. For instance, an abuser may take advantage of a single payment of a joint benefit claim by insisting that it is paid into their bank account; they may report a current/former partner for benefit or tax fraud; or they may take advantage of economic dependency created through immigration rules which require them to financially sponsor a spouse who has insecure status. An abuser might also refuse to give consent to close a joint financial product such as a bank account or sign up to a new fixed rate mortgage. Sometimes institutional economic abuse may not be inadvertent. A police officer might refuse to provide an escort to safely collect a victim's belongings if they leave (Sharp, 2008).

Victim-survivors describe expending considerable time and energy battling 'the system' and observe that their efforts to expand their economic space for action are not only constrained by the abuser, but also structural barriers (Kelly et al., 2014) as described above. Since dealing with abuse and its legacies is clearly not a linear journey, support needs to extend far beyond being enabled to separate.

The passage of the Domestic Abuse Act (2021) provided a mechanism within which to address this. With the support of the violence against women and girls' sector, SEA worked with peers and academics to call for the Act to amend section 76 of the Serious Crime Act (2015) and extend the CCB offence to apply in situations where a victim-survivor is no longer living and/or in a relationship with an abusive partner of family member. In March 2021, the Westminster Government accepted this amendment, and at the time of writing, the charity is contributing to work to amend the statutory guidance accordingly.

SUMMARY

This chapter has explored the definition of economic abuse set out in the Domestic Abuse Act (2021) to develop an understanding of the 'technology' that underpins it. That the concept of economic abuse continues to be redefined and expanded, reflects emerging scholarship on the issue (Sharp-Jeffs, 2021). Yet all behaviours sit within the overarching 'function of economic abuse as a mechanism of control'.

Moreover, it is recognised that although economic abuse might take the form of single incidents, this form of control is commonly a pattern of behaviour and is ongoing, including post-separation. In some cases, economic control is even transferred to the victim's children and family members in the aftermath of their death. This reinforces the importance of revisiting existing policy and legislation, as well as considering economic abuse in the development of new.

Based on critical analysis of each component part of the statutory definition, a revised working definition is put forward by Sharp-Jeffs (2021a):

> *'Economic abuse' means any behaviour (restriction, exploitation and/or sabotage) that has a substantial adverse effect on B's ability to acquire, use or maintain money or other property, goods, or services.*

The next chapter will further explore how economic abuse is experienced by victim-survivors with reference to personal, social and economic power.

NOTES

1. Domestic Abuse Act 2021 (legislation.gov.uk).

2. In a research report on child contact proceedings, four years later, women's experiences of economic abuse were explored, and the four broad forms were found to be present to varying degrees (Coy et al., 2011).

3. 'This is not love': victim of coercive control says she saw red flags from start | Domestic violence | The Guardian.

4. My abusive ex pawned my wedding ring, landed me with £80k debt and told me a double suicide was the only way out (thesun.co.uk).

5. In Focus: Not everyone survives domestic abuse | Metro News.

6. https://www.telegraph.co.uk/women/life/husband-saddled-80000-debt/.

7. Female Genital Mutilation Prosecution Guidance | The Crown Prosecution Service (cps.gov.uk).

8. 'My husband ran up a £58,000 debt in my name' - BBC News.

9. The Guardian view on predatory marriage: new safeguards are needed | Editorial | The Guardian.

10. Romance fraud: 'I wish I hadn't given £300k to a man I met online' - BBC News.

Chapter Two

HOW ECONOMIC ABUSE IS EXPERIENCED

This chapter considers how economic abuse is experienced by victim-survivors. It starts by exploring how abusers derive their power from structural inequalities linked to gender, socio-economic status, ethnicity, sexuality, disability and age. It recognises that, whilst anyone can experience economic abuse, the likelihood increases when an individual has fewer personal, social and economic resources. For this reason, individuals who experience intersecting inequalities are at particular risk. Abusers use their power to wear down a victim-survivors' resistance to coercive control through targeting these resources, thereby (further) reducing their space for action. The chapter concludes by considering the ripple effect of economic abuse (VonDeLinde & Sussman, 2017) in the short, medium and long terms. Based on this understanding, responses to economic abuse can then be developed.

PAYING ATTENTION TO SOCIAL CONTEXT

Abusers derive power from, and may take advantage of, structural inequalities. For instance, discussion of the Duluth Power and Control Wheel (Figure One) has illustrated how male privilege is used by men who control their intimate partners in heterosexual relationships. Victim-survivors of domestic abuse give examples of behaviours linked to this which include treating her like a servant; making all the big decisions; acting like the master of the castle; and being the one to define men's and women's roles.

Stark (2007) notes that traditional attitudes towards gender roles made possible by sexual inequality place men at a social and economic advantage. This helps explains why coercive control is hard to detect because the 'means and effects ... are easily confused with the range of sacrifices women are expected to make in their roles as homemakers, parents, and sexual partners' (Stark, 2007, p. 230). Beliefs about gender held by abusive men therefore converge with a discriminatory social context which is, in turn, reinforced through institutional structures and policies (as addressed within Chapter One).

DIFFERENT FORMS OF PRIVILEGE

Indeed, in conceptualising coercive control, Dutton and Goodman (2005) draw on theories of power that pay 'attention to the social context' and which highlight that not only does privilege arise in relation to gender, but also socio-economic status, ethnicity, sexuality, disability and age. The introductory chapter acknowledges that there is a limited evidence based on economic abuse as it is experienced by different groups meaning research is needed with a wider demographic sample (see Adams et al., 2019; Postmus et al., 2018; Singh, 2022). However, what is known about gender and how it intersects with other inequalities is outlined below.

Gender

Women's Experiences

The forerunner of the CSEW – the British Crime Survey – started to record data on financial and emotional abuse in 2001/2002. The surveys have consistently found that women are far more likely than men to have experienced non-physical forms of IPV (emotional and financial) (a) since the age of 16 and (b) at least once in the past year. The most recent data report (a) 17.2% and (b) 4.9% for women, compared to (a) 7.1% and (b) 2.2% for men (Stripe, 2020).

The methodology underpinning the CSEW reflects the Government's definition of domestic violence and is based on 'one or more' incidents of violence regardless of context (intent or impact). When patterns of abuse are explored, women are also more likely than men to say that they have experienced all forms of abuse asked about and to have experienced greater frequency and severity of violence. When the 'cap' on frequency of incidents[1] used within the CSEW methodology is removed, the estimate of violent crime that is committed against women increases still further (Walby, 2016).

These findings are reflected when gender is broken down within two nationally representative surveys undertaken by The Cooperative Bank/Refuge – one in 2015 and one in 2020. Women are disproportionately impacted by financial/economic abuse and are also more likely to report experiencing other forms of abuse, including higher rates of physical, emotional and sexual abuse compared to men (Butt, 2020; Sharp-Jeffs, 2015b). Furthermore, the 2015 survey found that women are more likely to experience financial abuse in multiple relationships as well as post-separation (one in four).

In many ways, this is unsurprisingly since progress towards achieving economic equality has been slow. Economic power used to be held by men by legal default (Littwin, 2012). It was only in 1964 that the Married Women's Property Act entitled a woman to keep half of any savings she had made from the allowance given to her by her husband. In 1970, the Equal Pay Act made it illegal for employers to pay women lower rates than men for the same work; yet at the same time working women could only secure a mortgage with the signature of a male guarantor. Indeed, women were unable to apply for a loan or credit in their own name until the Equal Credit Opportunity Act passed into law in 1974.[2]

Despite the many advances that women have and continue to make in the economic sphere, Wilcox (2006) observes how the labour market still reproduces differently gendered outcomes for men and women. On this basis, Anitha (2019) argues for a broadening out of economic abuse to encompass tasks, responsibilities and roles which are examples of economic activity, but which are not constructed in the same way as paid work. She observes that, through highlighting coercive control in the context of women's performance of their traditional gender roles, Stark (2007) drew 'welcome attention' to this realm, but that it has subsequently been neglected (Anitha, 2019, p. 1855).

Finances also continue to be gendered, with men still normatively expected to take charge of money (Postmus et al., 2018). So deeply are gendered concepts around the control of economic resources ingrained that, in an evaluation of 12 forms of abusive behaviour addressed via community-run perpetrator programmes, reduction was only marginal (3%) for 'tries to use money/finances to control me' over a 12-month period. This suggests that attitudes underpinning the control of economic resources may be particularly difficult to challenge and change (Kelly & Westmarland, 2015).

Outlined in the introductory chapter is the 'opposite' concept of coercive control – 'space for action' (Kelly, 2003). This term is used to describe a victim-survivors' autonomy or agency.[3] Kelly et al. (2014) developed scales for measuring coercive control and space for action and presented statistical evidence to show a significant correlation between the two – with high levels of coercive control resulting in low space for action and vice versa.

This is significant since the consequences of seeking to expand space for action by challenging coercive control can be 'too costly to pursue' for women (Stark, 2007, p. 235). The ultimate challenge to coercive control – separation or its threat – is when they are at highest risk of being killed. Data from the Homicide Index for the year ending March 2017 to the year ending March 2019 show that over three-quarters of victims of domestic homicide were female (ONS, 2019).

That men are not at the same risk of homicide as women leads Dutton and Goodman (2005, p. 746) to suggest that women and men 'may differ in their ability to convey a credible threat'. Similarly, Stark (2007) suggests that it is 'unusual' for women to be able to achieve the kind of dominance associated with coercive control within heterosexual relationships that men can.

Men's Experiences

In-depth work with male victims of IPV has suggested that there are 'certain circumstances' in which it may be possible for women to exert coercive control over men (Myhill, 2015). Certainly, this was illustrated by the male partner of the first woman prosecuted for CCB who spoke out publicly to highlight men's experiences and featured in a BBC3 documentary 'Abused by My Girlfriend'.[4]

As the previous chapter outlined, an abuser may take advantage of an existing imbalance of power, they may also seek to create a power imbalance where previously there was none. The fact that coercive control draws on personalised knowledge of a victim-survivors' resources and vulnerabilities (Stark, 2007; see also Kelly et al., 2014) is particularly relevant here. When attention is paid to individual and familial factors as well, it is possible to recognise that women can also be agents of coercion in intimate relationships (Dutton & Goodman, 2005). This includes same-sex relationships (see below).

The Cooperative Bank/Refuge 2015 survey data found that men were more likely to report financial abuse from women as single, exploitative incidents and were likely to experience it post-separation (one in five). Three-quarters reported that the onset of financial abuse was when they opened a joint bank account and half reported it starting when they bought a home with their partner (Sharp-Jeffs, 2015b).

Trans Identity

ONS data for the year ending March 2020 do not report on the experience of domestic abuse by trans identity. However, data collected by Galop's domestic abuse advocacy survey found that trans women disclosed the highest levels of financial abuse (30%) compared to trans men (3%; Magic & Kelley, 2018).

Class/Socio-economic Status

The ONS does not hold data specifically on social class either; however, it does provide a demographic breakdown of victims by characteristics such as, employment status, occupation and household income. This is interesting since Stark (2012) has suggested that one circumstance in which it may be possible for women to exert coercive control over men is when they enjoy an advantage based on social class or income.

For the year ending March 2020, the CSEW showed that, of adults aged 16–74 years, those who were unemployed were more likely to have experienced domestic abuse within the last year than those who were employed or economically inactive (Stripe, 2020).[5] For each occupation type except 'never-worked' and 'long-term unemployed', women were more likely to have experienced domestic abuse than men. This includes managerial/professional, intermediate and routine/manual occupations. The difference is greatest for full-time students, where 10.5% of women had experienced domestic abuse in the last year, compared with 4.8% of men (see below). It is suggested by the ONS that some of the differences seen by occupation type are also linked to age.

In terms of income, of adults aged 16–74 years, women are again more likely to experience domestic abuse across all income brackets. The difference is greatest for women who earn less than £10,000 (8.8% compared to 1.6%; Stripe, 2020). Of course, it may be the case that the low household income reported by some women may be a consequence of disrupted employment due to fleeing violence and setting up a new household as a lone parent without their ex-partner's income (Wilcox, 2006). It is also highlighted that survey findings should be treated cautiously since abused women living in more affluent households are 'slightly less likely' to define an event as domestic violence and are 'significantly less likely' to inform the police than those in poorer households – perhaps because they may experience more stigma attached to their abuse (Walby & Allen, 2004). This makes it 'hard to disentangle the direction of the causality, as to whether low income is a cause or consequence of domestic violence' (Walby & Allen, 2004, p. 75).

However, at the same time, men continue to have greater control over what Dobash and Dobash (1979) call the 'negotiation of daily life' due to factors such as the gender-pay gap or because women are in lower-paid roles, are working part-time or have stopped work due to childcare responsibilities. The Duluth Power and Control Wheel identifies that a common form of economic abuse is being given an allowance to be spent on household necessities and nothing more (Anderson et al., 2003; Postmus, Huang, & Mathisen-Stylianou, 2012a; Tolman, 1989). Frequently, the amount of money is inadequate, meaning that women are then forced to negotiate access to additional resources from a subordinate position (Dobash & Dobash, 1979; Littwin, 2012). This, in turn, may lead to other forms of abuse – for example, being given money by the perpetrator only if they perform sexual acts in return (Sharp, 2008).

CARING RESPONSIBILITIES

In her in-depth exploration of 'Marriage Money', Singh (1997) notes that, in cases where women's money comes from other sources, the traditional 'household allowance' system has given way to the 'shared' or 'independent management' systems. Under the shared management system, money is pooled into a joint bank account and responsibility for expenditure is shared. In contrast, the independent management system is one where both partners have their own money and pool part of their money into a joint account for household expenses.

Under the shared management system, Singh (1997) recognises that it is still possible for one partner to have greater control and influence over the way money is spent – usually (but not always) the person who earns most of it. This is because ownership of money is still associated with the earning of the money. For example, when a child is born then the father's influence relative to the mother's increases. This highlights how, despite the 'jointness' of a joint account, gender roles 'show the continuing strength of the more traditional view of man as the provider and woman as the homemakers and child-carer' (Singh, 1997, p. 72). The potential for 'trust' to be broken – through denial of access to money within a joint bank account – therefore continues to exist (see Cameron, 2014).

The Cooperative Bank/Refuge 2015 survey findings are consistent with this. Seven in ten women reported that the financial abuse they experienced began when they stopped working. Less than half of those surveyed and experiencing financial abuse were in full-time employment. The same number reported that they started to experience financial abuse when they had children (Sharp-Jeffs, 2015b). This is significant since pregnancy is a risk factor associated with domestic abuse. Brownridge, Tallieu, Tyler, Tiwari, and Chan (2011, p. 875) compared female victims of IPV who were and were not victimised during pregnancy and concluded: 'it is possible that economic subordination are potential warning signs of pregnancy violence'. It is certainly the case that women with children are disproportionately likely to experience economic abuse. Again, The Cooperative Bank/Refuge 2015 survey found that nearly three-quarters of economic abuse survivors have one or more children (Sharp-Jeffs, 2015b).

When Jaffe (2002) asked survivors of domestic violence who were also mothers to talk about the reasons why they had not left their violent partner earlier, they found that a central theme of their decision-making process had been concern about access to money and safe and affordable housing. This is consistent with the hypothesis that women find it harder to earn sufficient income to establish and maintain a new home if they have dependent children to support (Walby & Allen, 2004). Research by Women's Aid (2019) found that just under half of survivors reported struggling to have enough money to pay for essentials for their children after leaving.

This means that many abused women must balance the possible harm to themselves and any children they might have by living in far more basic conditions after leaving their partner against the harm that they may face either directly or indirectly from staying with him (Correia, 2000; Davis, 1999; Fender, Holmes, & Levy, 2002).

DISSOLVING RELATIONSHIPS

The Cooperative Bank/Refuge 2015 survey found that most women (78%) reported enduring financial abuse for more than five years before being able to leave (Sharp-Jeffs, 2015b). Indeed Anderson's (2007) exploration of the differential financial positioning of men and women in heterosexual relationships concluded that women's ability to dissolve relationships in which they are abused is constrained by the gendering of breadwinning responsibilities. Consequently, women who experience IPV have fewer economic resources on which to survive than men in the same situation. Furthermore, studies consistently demonstrate that, whilst most women and children will experience deterioration in their economic status in the year immediately following separation, men usually see an immediate improvement (Westaway & McKay, 2007).

Of those men who self-reported experiencing financial abuse in The Cooperative Bank/Refuge 2015 survey, six in ten stated the duration as being for six months or less (Sharp-Jeffs, 2015b). Again, this suggests that men generally have greater economic autonomy and are, therefore, able to separate more quickly. Seven in ten reported working full time and a third earned over £50,000. Men were also less likely to report experiencing financial abuse in a former relationship but were slightly more likely than women to have one or more children. However, fewer reported economic abuse starting when they had children (Sharp-Jeffs, 2015b).

As noted above, work with male victims of intimate partner abuse has suggested that, when a woman has a higher income or is from a higher social class, then it may be possible for her to exert coercive control over her partner (Myhill, 2015). Findings of The Cooperative Bank/Refuge 2015 survey found that 67% of men reported that financial abuse started when they retired and 65% when they experienced a drop in income.

Ethnicity

For the year ending March 2020, the CSEW showed that, of adults aged 16–74 years, mixed-race women are more likely to experience domestic abuse (9.4%), followed by white women (7.7%), black women (4.6%) and Asian women (4.4%; Stripe, 2020).

In The Cooperative Bank/Refuge 2015 survey, women and men who self-reported experiencing financial abuse were mostly white (91%; 89%). Women who had experienced financial abuse were slightly more likely to say that they were black and minoritised (6%) than men (4%). Men were slightly more likely to describe their ethnicity as mixed race (4%) than women (2%).

When Thiara and Gill (2012) explored the experience of domestic violence for South Asian and African Caribbean women they identified patterns of financial abuse which reflected the constructs of restriction and exploitation. Some women were being forced to live in total financial dependence and sometimes poverty (more common amongst South Asian women); whilst others reported men taking their money if they worked or were claiming benefits (more common amongst African Caribbean women).

Chowbey (2017) has also drawn on the constructs of economic abuse to understand the experiences of South Asian women. She combined the work of Adams et al. (2008) and Sharp (2008 – see Chapter One) when analysing interviews with 84 women from first and second generation British Pakistani Muslim ($n=23$) and British Gujarati Hindu ($n=12$) communities, as well as Gujarati Hindus in India ($n=26$) and Pakistani Muslims in Pakistan ($n=23$). More than one-third reported experiencing economic abuse ($n=33$).

However, Chowbey (2017) also identified what she describes as two 'unique' abuses. The first involved 'exploiting women's marriage gifts' – for example, threatening to throw them out of the house if they did not bring more dowry in the form of cash or household goods. Husbands (and sometimes mothers-in-law) also took control of gold (jewellery) for their own use. The second was 'jeopardising' women's long-term finances. In the British context, one of the most common forms of this was the abuser making transnational investments for themselves, their parents and siblings. Money, including for essential household expenses, was used for building properties 'back home'. This chimes with Singh's (2022) research into the experience of Anglo-Celtic and

Indian women in Australia, which also identified husbands demanding dowry and sending all his earnings, and some of hers, to his parents. As Chapter One notes, for some women, the abuser is not always their partner or husband, but family members including parents, siblings and in-laws.

Anitha (2019) similarly identified economic abuse in her study which drew on life-history interviews with 41 South Asian women in transnational marriages in the UK and India. However, she instead framed the 'particularities' she observed within her work under Postmus et al.'s (2016) three categories of economic control, economic exploitation and employment sabotage. The surreptitious or coercive sale of women's dowry (jewellery or other assets) alongside the taking away of customary gifts given to the victim was classified as a form of economic exploitation, whereas control over bank accounts (likely to be in the name of the male head of the household, often the father-in-law) was classified as economic control.

The approach taken by Anitha (2019) suggests that the constructs of economic abuse (restriction, exploitation and sabotage) can accommodate a wide variety of behaviours that interfere with a victim-survivors ability to acquire, use and maintain economic resources. This recognition is important since it may prevent practitioners from 'othering' women from different socio-economic and ethnic backgrounds through culturalising their experiences (see Thiara & Gill, 2010). This is discussed in more detail later on in the chapter.

Privilege arising from immigration status may also be used to control economic resources. The research evidence in relation to this has only explored women's experiences, although the nature of this power imbalance might also enable a woman to exert coercive control over a male partner.

Howard and Skipp (2015) undertook interviews and focus group discussions with survivors of financial abuse and documented how abusive men may exploit a woman's immigration status to perpetrate financial abuse. This control is facilitated by a system that requires the resident with permanent residency to financially sponsor their partner until they too receive leave to remain – what Sharp (2008) describes in Chapter One as a form of institutional economic abuse and the significance of which is set out in more detail within Chapter Four.

Singh (2022) also notes how conditions attached to temporary non-partner visas restrict migrant women's access to help with housing, finance and health services in Canada. Poverty, low socio-economic status and belonging to a cultural, racial or ethnic minority increases the difficulty of victim-survivors trying to achieve economic independence (Peled & Krigel, 2016).

Tactics may include misinforming a partner about benefit and banking systems claiming that, as the British partner, the abuser should claim child benefit or suggesting that the sponsored partner is unable to open a bank account. Barriers to support increase if migrant women do not have fluency in English (Singh, 2022). Littwin (2012) also notes coerced debt cases in which the abuser makes their partner sign financial documents that they cannot read or provides a 'mis-translation' of the contents.

Sexuality

Overarching CSEW data show that, for the year ending March 2020, of adults aged 16–74 years, bisexual women (19.6%) are more likely to experience domestic abuse. This is followed by those whose sexual orientation is gay/lesbian (12.2%) and then heterosexual (6.9%; Stripe, 2020).

Data specific to financial abuse collected by The Cooperative Bank/Refuge 2015 survey found that most people (88%)

who self-reported experiencing an incident of financial abuse were heterosexual, 5% were in same-sex relationships and 5% reported being bisexual. At the same time, men in same-sex relationships reported experiencing disproportionately higher levels of economic abuse compared to women in same-sex relationships (Sharp-Jeffs, 2015b).

This contrasts with the findings of Galop's domestic abuse advocacy survey which found that, by sexual orientation, lesbian women disclosed the highest levels of financial abuse (16%) compared to gay (13%) and bisexual clients (2%; Magic & Kelley, 2018).

Disability

For the year ending March 2020, of adults aged 16–74 years, CSEW data show that disabled women (14.7%) are more likely than not disabled women (6%) to experience domestic abuse; but that disabled men (7.5%) are more likely than not disabled women (3.2%) to experience domestic abuse (Stripe, 2020).

Again, this contrasts with The Cooperative Bank/Refuge 2015 survey findings specific to financial abuse. Whilst there were more disabled women in the sample who experienced financial abuse than men, the proportion of men who self-reported being disabled was higher compared to women (Sharp-Jeffs, 2015b).

Hague, Thiara, and Magowan (2007) explored the experiences of disabled women and found that they experienced 'particular' forms of financial abuse. These included abusive men using their partner's personal disability allowances and payments and denying women money for their prescriptions, as well as essential personal needs related to their condition. Women were remonstrated for not 'pulling their weight' and made to feel that because of their disability, they contributed little to the household. Within recommendations based on their research, Hague et al. (2007, p. 87) stated that, disabled women's experience of intimate violence 'may particularly include financial abuse and sexual and psychological violence'.

Age

Young women experience the highest rates of domestic abuse than any age group, simply because they tend to have more relationships than older women who may be living with a partner or married. CSEW data show that 14% of young women aged 16–19 experience domestic abuse, with the second largest group (10%) being women aged 20–24 (Stripe, 2020).

Yet despite this, young women are the least likely to experience economic abuse compared to other age groups. A possible explanation for this is found in both The Cooperative Bank/Refuge 2015 and 2020 survey findings (Butt, 2020; Sharp-Jeffs, 2015b). These indicate that women's experiences of financial abuse coincide with key life stage events such as those outlined above within the discussion on 'shared' management systems for joint finances. In addition to stopping working and having children, events include getting married or moving in together – times at which a partner may insist on joint finances and the closing of an individual's bank account account to 'prove their commitment'. This is reflected in the 2015 statistics showing that 58% of financial abuse victim-survivors are either living with a partner (17%) or married/in a civil partnership (41%).

As such almost half (47%) of women who have experienced financial abuse are aged 30–49 compared to 0.5% who are 20 or younger (Sharp-Jeffs, 2015b). Young men under the age of 20 are highly unlikely to report economic abuse (0.25%; Sharp-Jeffs, 2015b). Younger women who do experience financial abuse tend to be in relationships with older partners and at greater risk due to the power imbalance of age (Barter, McCarry, Berridge, & Evans, 2009).

At the same time, however, the efforts of young people to develop economic independence may be limited by a partner controlling their ability to study. Again, in The Cooperative Bank/Refuge 2015 survey, 9% of women stated that their partner had interfered with their ability to go to college/university and 7% had been made to give up college/university (Sharp-Jeffs, 2015b). A study by the National Union of Students (NUS, 2011) reported that 2% of women students reported that someone had threatened to withhold the financial support that they needed to be a student. This is significant since, in a study examining the impact of a financial literacy programme on survivors of IPV there was a correlation between economic control and education level; the higher women's education level, the least amount of economic control the women experienced, suggesting that education is a protective factor (Postmus et al., 2012b).

A third of women (33%) in The Cooperative/Refuge 2015 survey who report experiencing financial abuse are older – between the ages of 50 and 69 (Sharp-Jeffs, 2015b). Bows (2015) explored how older women (those over 40) made decisions about reporting abuse to the police. Her findings suggested that the 'patterning' of abuse may change over the length of a relationship, with physical abuse decreasing and emotional, financial and sexual abuse increasing over time. Older women may not disclose IPV for several different reasons – lack of experience of work outside the home or access to independent economic resources being one (LGA and ADASS, 2015). Older women also have less time to 'start-over' and the prospect of claiming benefits, relying on a state pension (if they are indeed eligible – see Chapter Four), being responsible for money (perhaps for the first time) or coping with new ways of banking, such as online, may be too overwhelming (Portas & Sharp-Jeffs, 2021).

A DHR case analysis showed that it was common for professionals to make assumptions about age, with indicators of abuse presumed to be the result of stress arising from a partner having to take on a caring role arising from health needs, rather than the result of ongoing domestic abuse that may have been taking place for many decades (Sharp-Jeffs & Kelly, 2016).

INTERSECTIONALITY

The research evidence presented above shows that individuals who experience intersecting inequalities are at particular risk. The concept of intersectionality is, therefore, crucial to understanding who is at risk of economic abuse and how it is experienced.

The term intersectionality is attributed to the work of Kimberlé Crenshaw (1993) and recognises that an individual's experiences are shaped by multiple forms of oppression. Crenshaw (1993) draws on gender, race and class to demonstrate how 'structural intersectionality' makes the experience of domestic abuse qualitatively different for black and minoritised women compared to that of white women.

She illustrates this by drawing on the 'waiver for hardship caused by domestic violence' within the US Immigration and Nationality Act (1990). This provides that an abused spouse who has conditional permanent resident status can be granted a waiver to meet the requirements of remaining 'properly' married for two years before applying for permanent resident status if she can show that she was physically abused or subjected to extreme mental cruelty by a US citizen or permanent resident spouse. However, in practice, many immigrant women are unable to meet the conditions established to access these provisions, because they face obstacles in accessing the evidence required. For example, isolation and language barriers mean that some women will not have had contact with statutory agencies and been able to disclose the abuse that they were experiencing. Patterns of subordination intersect so that women are positioned to 'absorb the simultaneous impact of anti-immigration policy and their spouses' abuse' (Crenshaw, 1993, p. 1250). Thus, in developing a legal remedy that does not consider the intersectional location of black and minoritised women, Crenshaw shows how legislation intended to be available to 'all women' is 'made inaccessible to some'.

In writing about intersectionality, Kelly (2013, p. 2) highlights that it is important to recognise that layers of inequality are 'not simply additive'. This means that gender plus race plus class does not result in black and minoritised women being equally marginalised; this reproduces stereotypical representations of black and minoritised women and girls reflected within the 'cultural differences approach' to domestic abuse. In addition, the simple additive response encourages the construction of what Barnes and Mercer (2010, p. 85) label a 'misleading league table of oppressions'. This is illustrated by Begum (1992) who describes how the 'double oppression' of being a black woman may 'yield' to the 'triple oppression' of being a disabled, black woman.

In practice, these dimensions are not 'separate' oppressions but are interlocking and complex and mean that individuals will be situated in powerful/less ways to one another (Begikhani, Gill, & Hague, 2015).

Each axis signifies a specific modality of power relations. Specific articulations are produced through the way in which the different fields of power 'collide, enmesh and configure' (Brah, 1996, p. 248). Brah calls this a 'multiaxiality' of power within which race, gender and class as well as disability (and other protected characteristics) cannot be 'separated out'. Not only does this recognise 'differential positionings' but also how, in specific historical situations, there is 'differential access' to economic, political and cultural resources' (Yuval-Davis, 2006, p. 199) – what Thiara and Gill (2010) describe as the 'racial equality approach'.

It follows that when the intersection of multiple oppressions increases marginalisation, access to economic, social and personal resources is decreased, restricting equal options to safety and economic security (VonDeLinde & Sussman, 2017). The role of economic, social and personal resources is, therefore, significant and is explored next.

ECONOMIC, SOCIAL AND PERSONAL RESOURCES

To recap: abusers take advantage of the power they hold through different forms of privilege. They seek to reinforce and further their power as well as create a power imbalance where previously there was none. This makes responding to economic abuse challenging since there is no simple link between increasing economic security and decreasing violence.

In fact, for women, as Kelly (2011) observes, the reverse seems to be the case. Research suggests that a woman's higher income is associated with increased frequency of abuse (Turell, 2000). The Nordic countries, for example, are consistently rated at the top of all conventional measures of gender equality (equal pay and paid employment) yet the levels of violence against women are as high, and on some measurements, higher than in countries where less progress has been made (Kelly, 2011). In addition, abusers are significantly more likely to kill female partners in transient societies where women have begun to enter the workforce (World Health Organisation, 2002) and in cities where women experience relatively high economic status compared to men (Stark, 2007). This leads Walby and Allen (2004, p. 73) to suggest that a causal link for violence may be via the perpetrator who, unable to 'perform masculinity to his satisfaction' uses physical violence to 'obtain a source of power that is otherwise not obtainable' (Walby & Allen, 2004, p. 90).

Within Chapter One's discussion on interfering with a woman's ability to acquire, use or maintain economic resources, the scenario in which men 'refuse to contribute' to household expenses is discussed in relation to creating economic insecurity. Littwin (2012, p. 981) describes this as women being forced into a position of 'supplication' (solely responsible for paying rent/mortgage, utility bills, food, toiletries and clothing)[6] and suggests that this behaviour may 'reflect the ways in which abusive men have had to adapt their attempts to control women because of the financial advances that women have made over the past forty years'. From this perspective, she writes, economic abuse is a 'patriarchal phenomenon' intended to 'wage war on women's growing equality'. Dutton and Goodman (2005) describe this as 'wearing down resistance'. Compliance with coercive demands may be more likely when there are fewer resources to combat the pressure of doing so.

'WEARING DOWN RESISTANCE'

Chapter One focussed in considerable detail on control over 'tangible' resources in the form of economic resources. However, through also drawing out how economic abuse is connected to other forms of abuse (see, for example, Figure Two – the Economic Power and Control Wheel), it is clear how this behaviour can reduce a victim-survivors' access to personal and social resources too, narrowing their space for action still further. Dutton and Goodman (2005) define social resources as 'emotional support from friends, family and work colleagues, the absence of which can create futility and despair'. Personal resources are described as 'physical stamina, determination, willingness to take risks'.

Maslow's hierarchy of needs is useful in developing an understanding of this from a psychological perspective. According to Maslow, some needs such as those for food, water and shelter are basic to survival (physiological). They energise a person and direct their behaviour until they are met. Next activated (building up from the bottom) are safety needs for security and protection (such as employment, housing and money), followed by love or belonginess (closeness and affiliation with other people) and then esteem needs which include love and respect. Finally, at the top of the hierarchy (the highest level) are self-actualisation needs which enable an individual to actualise their self-potential (see Westen, 1996).

Whilst control over economic resources in meeting both physiological and safety needs is explicit, economic resources are also implicitly linked to the higher levels. Isolation through control over economic resources such as mobile phones, computers, the internet and a car, takes away the ability to connect to friends and family (Kelly et al., 2014; Singh, 2020). It is also difficult to imagine how an individual can develop self-esteem and fulfil their potential if they are constantly degraded. Research commonly notes how women are denied access to sanitary products (Butt, 2020; Women's Aid, 2015, 2019) or, in one case, made to eat supper on the floor from a dog bowl (Wiener, 2017).

THE IMPACT OF ECONOMIC ABUSE

Consideration of Maslow's hierarchy also links into consideration of the range of impacts that economic control has on victim-survivors. Given the way that economic abuse threads through coercive control, it may be difficult to disentangle these from the impact of other forms of abuse (Macdonald, 2012). However, they can broadly be grouped into three areas: economic security; emotional/psychological wellbeing; and physical wellbeing.

Economic Security

Linked to the immediate impact of lacking the resources required for day-to-day survival (see Chapter One) is the possibility that the victim-survivor may be unable to budget and manage any money they do have/receive because they were prevented from doing so by the abuser (Barron, 2012; Howard & Skipp, 2015). The association between economic abuse and psychological abuse means that victim-survivors may also lack self-confidence in their ability to deal with financial matters independently (Howard & Skipp, 2015; Stark, 2007; VonDeLinde & Correia 2005).

Victim-survivors may be in debt (mortgages, rent, credit cards, payday loans, utility bills, hire purchase contracts, mobile phone plans, parking fines, etc.) because of economic abuse and see their income reduced because of the repayments they must make every month (Sharp, 2008). Women report being left with higher levels of debt because of economic abuse compared to male victim-survivors and are much more likely to say that they are still paying off debt incurred in their name by a partner sometime after leaving (54% of women, compared to 29% of men – Butt, 2020).

In addition to discovering existing debts, victim-survivors may experience post-separation abuse so that new debts may be created. For example, the perpetrator may withdraw all the funds from bank accounts that they continue to have access to (Robinson, 2003; Wilcox, 2006) and may increase and/or spend a joint overdraft (Howard & Skipp, 2015). Victim-survivors may be unable to pay the debts they are left with (Howard & Skipp, 2014; Smallwood, 2015) and, in some cases, this may result in insolvency and bankruptcy (Branigan, 2004; Stark, 2007). If a victim-survivors' financial standing has been destroyed by an abusive ex-partner, then it will be particularly difficult to access credit and mainstream financial services that would help enable them to become self-sufficient (Corrie & McGuire, 2013; Littwin, 2012).

Research shows that women are generally more likely to experience financial hardship post-separation compared to men (Westaway & McKay, 2007). However, where economic abuse occurs, this can be magnified. Adams et al. (2008) present research to suggest that there is a particular link between economic abuse and economic hardship where women who experience higher levels of economic abuse place greater responsibility for their economic hardships on their experience (see also, VonDeLinde & Sussman, 2017).

Certainly, a report by Portas and Sharp-Jeffs (2021) suggests that economic abuse compounds the risks girls and women already face throughout their financial life course. Through presenting data and insights about economic abuse across '6 Moments that Matter' (developed by Portas, 2020)[7] they show how abusers may seek to exercise control that not only negatively impacts their future economic security, but also how decisions taken in the immediate, short and even medium term are interlinked with longer term consequences. For example, immediate need for money due to economic abuse may result in a victim-survivor making a decision that impacts a future divorce settlement and their pension income.

> **CASE STUDY SEVEN:** Joy's Story – Socio-economic Status.
>
> When I left my ex-partner, I had to change my work arrangements. I was offered early retirement at 57 years old due to ill health. I had the choice of taking a large lump sum of money and a low monthly life-time payment or a lower lump sum and a higher monthly lifetime sum. I couldn't ask anybody at work because I didn't want to admit what I was going through, nor could I talk to the pension services about other options because I felt they wouldn't have understood my situation. In normal circumstances I would have taken the latter option, but as I was not able to work, and the abuser was not working I took the large lump sum option. Later, when we divorced, the lump sum and its use was not considered in the financial arrangements.

This is borne out by the experience of victim-survivors with financial difficulties, supported by the MAP casework service. The service reports that women dip in and out at different points in their journey and when their circumstances change, for example, when they need to negotiate their share of equity in the matrimonial home or claim a separate pension (Barron, 2012). It also draws attention to the need for coordinated and integrated responses to victim-survivors of economic abuse, a theme which is revisited in Chapter Five which sets out future directions.

New dangers arise from not responding to the economic needs of victim-survivors. Some may resort to criminal activity such as shoplifting (Sharp, 2008) or seek money from doorstep lenders or payday loan companies. They may be targeted by unscrupulous landlords offering to accept sex for rent or feel that they must move in with a new partner sooner than would have otherwise been the case, for financial reasons.

Emotional/Psychological Wellbeing

The psychological impact and overlaps with emotional/psychological abuse (Chapter One) mean economic abuse is associated with depression, anxiety and reduced quality of life (Adams & Beeble, 2019; Postmus et al., 2012a).

Cameron (2014) observes that intimate partner abuse takes place in a complex context where emotions of love, trust and commitment converge with social expectations and norms for intimate relationships. For instance, a joint bank account is 'a symbol of trust' representing a jointness through marriage (Singh, 1997). Victim-survivors share that, when they realise that their partner has economically abused them, this triggers conflicting emotions (Cameron, 2014; Sharp-Jeffs, 2008) and that leaving and working though the implications can be emotionally draining. In other research, women have also reported finding it difficult to trust that this will not happen in future relationships (Howard & Skipp, 2015, see Case Study Two, Amy's story).

Economic abuse may also affect psychological health through the stress associated with poverty and facing an uncertain financial future (Adams et al., 2008; Howard & Skipp, 2015; Macdonald, 2012; Smallwood, 2015). This may be exacerbated through substandard housing, inadequate food and unstable income. Consistent with research on debt more broadly, victim-survivors also report that this is an emotional toll; however, this is again compounded by the particularity of the context in which the debt was accrued. As well as feelings of betrayal, victim-survivors share a sense of injustice – being required to pay back debt that was taken out without their consent, facing bankruptcy and having a ruined credit rating because of the actions of the abuser (Sharp, 2008; Smallwood, 2015). For victim-survivors who are paying back debt, every payment is a reminder of the abuser they experienced – something that creditors should consider when responding to customers in this situation (see Chapter Four).

All this is reflected within the case studies shared, making it easy to relate to why victim-survivors may self-harm. Alcohol and drug dependency are another means of coping with domestic violence and may even be encouraged by the abuser as this may act as another impediment to employment (Lloyd & Taluc, 1999; US General Accounting Office, 1998; Wilcox, 2006). Such coping strategies may result in early death as was sadly the case for Emily and even suicide. Indeed, more women take their own lives as an escape from abuse than those who are killed by a current/former partner (Walby & Allen, 2004).

Lodge (2020) believes that, when set against the backdrop of action taken to address domestic abuse, it 'seems paradoxical that domestic abusers whose conduct precipitates a victim's suicide have thus far managed to evade the full rigour of the criminal law's prohibitions against harmful conduct'. In her paper on domestic abuse and suicide she refers to the experience of Gurjit Dhaliwal who took her own life following years of psychological, and occasionally physical, abuse perpetrated by her husband. He limited who she was allowed to see, when she could go out, what she wore and when she went to work. In 2006, the CPS with the support of Refuge and Southall Black Sisters, attempted to hold Gurjit's husband criminally liable for her suicide. However, the case collapsed. The decisive issue was whether grievous bodily harm required a finding that the victim had been caused to suffer a recognised psychiatric illness, or whether the infliction of serious psychological illness or injury would suffice to ground the manslaughter charge. The Court of Appeal upheld the trial judge's determination that nothing short of recognised psychiatric harm or injury would constitute 'bodily harm' in this context.

Justene Reece took her own life as a 'direct result' of the controlling behaviour that she experienced from her ex-boyfriend. He tracked her movements and sometimes stopped her from going out by physically throwing her to the floor or, on two occasions, putting his hands around her neck.[8] After dating him for a year, she fled to a refuge where he tried to find her. He made 3,500 attempts to contact her via calls, texts and social media messages and stalked those people who were close to her, including her employer. It was later discovered that he had numerous previous convictions for offences committed against women. These included threatening to set fire to the house of one victim-survivor's father.[9] Nicholas Allen pleaded guilty to a charge of manslaughter, controlling and coercive behaviour and six counts of stalking. A consultant psychiatrist who reviewed all the evidence and medical records said she had been in a 'substantially abnormal' mental state, suffering from depression, panic attacks and feelings of hopelessness.[10] However, because the guilty plea precluded any detailed discussion of the offence requirements many questions remain unanswered regarding the scope of liability for manslaughter in these circumstances (Lodge, 2020).

Physical Health

In addition to being a risk marker for domestic abuse, with victim-survivors twice as likely to be in arrears and to have had to borrow money to pay for essential items (Wilcox, 2006), poverty associated with economic abuse is yet another predictor of adverse health impacts (Singh, 2022).

This chapter outlined the links between economic abuse and physical wellbeing. The Economic Power and Control Wheel illustrates how attempts to challenge economic abuse may lead to physical violence, including threats to kill and, in some, cases homicide.

Physical injuries may also arise from economic control. Examples include victims-survivors not being allowed to use the car and therefore having to carry heavy bags of groceries, or not being allowed to turn on the heating, leading to arthritis and asthma due to the damp (Sharp, 2008). In addition to chronic pain, the long-term physical effects of abuse may include damaged hearing and eyesight and this, in turn, can, impede the ability of victims-survivors to work (Brandwein, 1999).

SUMMARY

This chapter focussed on how economic abuse is experienced by victim-survivors by exploring the different ways in which power can be derived from a range of structural inequalities, including gender and how it intersects with sexuality, socio-economic status, ethnicity, disability and age. Attention was given to how abusers use their power to wear down a victim-survivors' resistance to coercive control. The repercussions of economic abuse, outlined in Chapter One, were built upon, moving beyond the immediate impact to focus on short-/medium-/long-term economic security, as well as emotional/psychological and physical wellbeing.

Part Two of this book takes the understanding of economic abuse built up in Chapters One and Two and considers how this can be integrated into responses, through the CCR model and interventions by the stakeholders within it.

NOTES

1. The CSEW cap of frequency of incidents is five.

2. Women and Credit Through the Decades: The 1970s - NerdWallet.

3. Inspired by Lundgren's (1998) earlier work on 'women's life space'.

4. Abused By My Girlfriend: Alex Skeel feared his partner Jordan Worth would kill him - BBC Three.

5. Domestic abuse victim characteristics, England and Wales – Office for National Statistics (ons.gov.uk).

6. Clothing (see also Adams et al., 2008; Branigan, 2004; Brewster, 2003; Citizen's Advice, 2014; Davies & Lyon, 1998; Howard & Skipp, 2015; Littwin, 2012; Ptacek, 1999; Sharp, 2008).

7. Growing up, studying and requalifying; entering and re-entering the workplace; relationships, making up and breaking up; motherhood, becoming a mother/carer; after life, planning and entering retirement; ill-health, infirmity and dying.

8. Man jailed for manslaughter over ex-girlfriend's suicide - BBC News.

9. Police failed stalking victim who killed herself, watchdog finds | UK news | The Guardian.

10. Man jailed for manslaughter over ex-girlfriend's suicide - BBC News.

PART TWO

RESPONDING TO ECONOMIC ABUSE

Chapter Three

THE COORDINATED COMMUNITY RESPONSE MODEL

Now that economic abuse is named and defined within national legislation and also recognised post-separation, this new understanding needs to be translated into policy and practice frameworks. This chapter explores the potential of the coordinated community response (CCR) model to do this. It suggests that this framework needs to be broadened to embrace 'non-traditional' stakeholders and sectors that have, up until now, been viewed as part of the 'wider support sector' if economic abuse is to be effectively addressed. This will enable the CCR to maximise spaces within which victim-survivors can speak out, ensure that they are supported and hold abusers to account. The chapter ends by outlining the component parts that underpin the CCR and considers how economic abuse can be incorporated into each. This 'sets the scene' for Chapter Four which explores the role of different sectors and stakeholders in more detail.

THE CCR TO DOMESTIC ABUSE

The multi-faceted nature of domestic abuse and its impacts means that coordinated approaches are needed to address it. Such approaches emphasise collaborative and integrated policy and practice frameworks which include all relevant sectors and stakeholders (Lovett, Coy, & Kelly, 2011). Without a CCR, sectors and stakeholders work in silos and adopt different approaches. This hinders prevention and early intervention work, means that victim-survivors struggle to navigate the services they need to support them and fails to hold perpetrators to account (STADA, 2020).

One of the earliest CCR models to domestic abuse emerged in Duluth Minnesota and has gone on to have global reach. It sets out a unified system of supports and sanctions with the safety of victim-survivors at the centre (Shepard, 1999). What makes it a CCR is that domestic violence is framed as the exercise of power and control and a cause and a consequence of gender inequality. Change, therefore, must extend beyond individual cases to institutions and communities to transform norms and practices. For instance, it is not enough to reform the law to criminalise domestic abuse if criminal justice agencies fail to implement legislation and hold abusers accountable, if they do not link into services providing protection, support and assistance to victim-survivors, or if communities resist changes to women's legal rights (Lovett et al., 2011).

The concept of a CCR was introduced to the UK through work undertaken by the London Borough of Hammersmith and Fulham in 1989 via what became known as a Domestic Violence Forum (Holder, 1999). Several hundred fora now exist across England and Wales. Over the years, their scope has expanded with many broadening their response to address different and connected forms of VAWG.

The charity, Standing Together Against Domestic Abuse (STADA), is the coordinating agency for the CCR nationally. It operates across a range of settings including, the criminal justice system, health, housing, social care and the wider community and works collaboratively with statutory and third sector partner agencies to create systemic change. This work has informed the development and implementation of interventions such as Specialist Domestic Violence Courts (SDVCs), Independent Domestic Violence Advisers (IDVAs) and Multi-Agency Risk Assessment Conferences (MARACs).[1] STADA also provides support in the operation of DHRs – a practical illustration of what may happen in the absence of a functioning CCR (STADA, 2020).

In practice, work with the community has largely been confined to professionals in specialist domestic abuse charities working with statutory agencies (Holder, 1999). Moreover, none of these approaches have, to date, integrated strategies that address the economic aspects of abuse. For example, a scoping study on economic advocacy across three local authority areas found the focus on immediate risk of physical harm within the MARAC process precluded economic safety. Economic abuse was described as likely to be a 'small footnote' in cases referred to the MARAC and not as central as it should be. Although reports of rent arrears and debt were quite common, agencies were said to 'steer away' from focussing on these issues, despite the interconnections (SEA, 2017, p. 18).

An analysis of 40 DHRs that had been quality assured by the Home Office Quality Assurance (QA) Panel between January 2013 and March 2016 was undertaken using a framework developed and widely used in the health context for understanding adverse events (Home Office, 2016). The framework addressed seven broad categories of factors, including the individuals involved in the case. Despite 13 cases of IPV and 3 cases of familial violence featuring 'employment issues' and 12 cases of IPV and 2 cases of familial violence featuring 'financial issues' there was no further exploration of either.

This contrasts with an exploratory study of seven intimate partner homicides in 'Engleshire' (Regan, Kelly, Morris, & Dibb, 2007). The study was undertaken because, unusually, there had been no prior statutory agency involvement with the cases. Thus, its aim was to examine what families and wider informal networks knew about the couple during the period leading up to the victim-survivors' death. This uncovered financial problems in three of the cases and in two cases there were 'severe debts'. In fact, family and friends in one case were aware that the victim-survivor had attended a consultation with a debt counselling service. The authors concluded that 'the presence of debt in half of these cases suggests these agencies should be part of domestic violence forums and coordinated community responses' (Regan et al., 2007, p. 28).

WHO DO VICTIM-SURVIVORS OF ECONOMIC ABUSE TELL?

Consistent with all forms of domestic abuse, the majority of those experiencing financial abuse were most likely to tell someone in their informal networks. Two-thirds of economic abuse victim-survivors report sharing their experience with a friend, family member or, to a lesser extent, a work colleague. Those who report formally are more likely to tell a bank or a money/debt advice service than a specialist domestic abuse service or statutory agencies such as a GP, the police, a social worker or another professional. Given that abusers use financial products and systems to control their partners, it is, perhaps, not surprising that victims-survivors are more likely to disclose in these spaces after family, friends and colleagues.

Women make up two-thirds of victim-survivors who disclose to no one. That women are less likely to disclose financial abuse suggests that they may be subject to a high level of control and/or be more fearful of the consequences of doing so (Sharp-Jeffs, 2015b). It may also be linked to findings which suggest that a barrier to formally reporting economic abuse includes not wanting the abuser to get a criminal record that might affect their job prospects (Westmarland, 2015). Indeed, the police may even discourage a victim-survivor from making a formal complaint for this reason (see Sharp, 2008). This concern reflects women's lesser economic independence and how they and any children they might have would struggle to survive if their partner was prosecuted and lost their job.

This latter point chimes with findings which show that, although women and men across all income levels report experiencing financial abuse, almost equal numbers of women and men earning over £50,001 are more likely to tell someone than those in lower income bands. This was also true of women and men living in a household with an income of over £50,001 (Sharp-Jeffs, 2015b). Explanations here might include that higher earning women/men have the economic means to support themselves independently and so the 'economic risk' of reporting is less. They might also be more likely to report economic abuse because they have greater economic assets to lose.

The finding that victim-survivors are least likely to disclose economic abuse to domestic abuse charities suggests a very low level of awareness that economic resources can be used as a source of power. This is concerning given that it has been suggested that economic abuse might precede physical violence within patterns of coercive control (Dobash & Dobash, 1980 cited by Howard & Skipp, 2010). If this is indeed the case, then ensuring that all relevant sectors and stakeholders are part of responses to domestic abuse is even more urgent.

EMBRACING 'NON-TRADITIONAL' SECTORS AND STAKEHOLDERS

Macdonald (2012, p. 21) observes the consequences of key institutions not 'being ready' to address domestic abuse means that they lag behind 'that which would be required to achieve significant positive action to address the problem'. Not only does this mean that opportunities to maximise spaces within which victim-survivors can speak out are lost, but there is a lack of support for victim-survivors and perpetrators are able to continue to use institutional systems to undertake abuse with impunity.

For this reason, to effectively address economic abuse, the CCR should incorporate new membership by extending the sectors and stakeholders with which it works (see also Sharp-Jeffs, 2016a) and move away from the approach advocated by Women's Aid (2019) that certain support needs are accessed from outside of the specialist domestic abuse service support network.

In relation to economic abuse, this means working with stakeholders in private sector organisations. This follows practice in Australia which locates responses to economic abuse within a cross-sectoral response that includes the financial services sector, utilities and essential service providers; telecommunications companies; regulators and ombudsman services; and the legal sector (Camilleri et al., 2015; Smallwood, 2015).

RECOGNISING DOMESTIC ABUSE AS AN ECONOMIC SAFETY ISSUE

Chapter Two outlined how there is a complex relationship between domestic abuse and economic safety. Lack of economic resources reduces safety options and creates increased vulnerability to violence. At the same time, domestic abuse creates economic insecurity for survivors (VonDeLinde & Sussman, 2017).

Addressing structural issues such as economic equality within the CCR has the potential to be preventative, better enabling victim-survivors to access protection and creating redress in the aftermath of abuse, supporting victim-survivors to rebuild their lives safely. One way of approaching this is to systematically integrate strategies on promoting economic safety into the 12 components of the CCR model (STADA, 2020). These are outlined below, along with suggestions about how this might be achieved in practice, thereby 'setting the scene' for Chapter Four which explores the role of different sectors and stakeholders in more detail.

1. Survivor Voice

Stakeholder responses to domestic abuse must be informed by the experiences of victim-survivors if their needs are to be met and they are to stay engaged. Historically, however, local areas have tended to consult only with women who are engaging with refuges or other domestic abuse services. Whilst there are benefits to this approach, many survivors, particularly those from minoritised groups, may not access these spaces. Therefore, this approach limits the voices of a diverse group of victim-survivors (STADA, 2020). Alternative approaches may include consulting women who are accessing healthcare services, for example. An evaluation by SafeLives to assess the impact of locating IDVAs in hospitals revealed that they were more likely to engage with groups of victims less visible to local specialist services, including individuals from high income households (SafeLives, 2016).

2. Intersectionality

Very closely linked to survivor voice is another component of the CCR – intersectionality (see Chapter Two). Through adopting an intersectional analysis when responding to domestic abuse, it is possible to analyse the ways in which individuals experience violence; the options open to them in dealing with that violence; and the extent to which they have access to services to help them (Thiara & Gill, 2010). The absence of an intersectional lens through which to analyse the experiences of victim-survivors – including class – may explain why limited consideration has been given to how availability of and control over economic resources will either enable or limit the options of victim-survivors; and how some groups may be at disproportionate risk of economic abuse than others (see Chapter Two).

Part two of the Equalities Act (2010)[2] recognises different forms of oppression as protected characteristics. When making decisions of a strategic nature, part one introduces a duty on the public sector to have 'due regard to the desirability of exercising them in a way that is designed to reduce the inequalities of outcome which result from socio-economic disadvantage'. However, over 10 years later, this provision has not yet been implemented – another contributing factor to its absence in policy and practice discussions.

3. Shared Objective

A theory of change is a useful tool that many local partnerships use to develop a shared objective. It describes the need (problems) that stakeholders are trying to address, the changes they want to make (outcomes) and what they plan to do (activities) to achieve this. Economic abuse may appear within the following:

- *Problem statements*: for example, victim-survivors lack the economic resources they need to leave an abusive partner and so stay longer and experience more harm; and victim-survivors experience economic abuse post-separation, making it difficult to rebuild their life independently and so may return to the abuser.

- *Activities*: for example, all agencies will screen for economic abuse and work with a victim-survivor to delink financially from an abuser and maximise their access to and control over economic resources; a flexible funding programme will be introduced enabling victim-survivors to pay off rent arrears accrued by an abusive partner (see Chapter Five).

- *Outcomes*: for example, victim-survivors have access to the economic resources they need to leave an abusive partner when they want to; victim-survivors will be able to stay in their own accommodation.

4. Structure and Governance

It is through governance structures that a shared objective can be agreed upon and then implemented. Again, good governance should reflect need, reinforcing the importance of survivor voice. An operational group linked to economic safety could sit under and feed up into the work of the strategic board. It could be jointly led by strategic partners such as a local specialist domestic abuse service and a debt/money advice service.

5. Strategy and Leadership

Any strategy must be developed with reference to the national policy and legislative landscape, meaning that the new statutory definition of domestic abuse – which includes economic abuse – should be adopted. It should also reflect the local context, for example, the socio-economic status of those who live in the local authority area. Prevention and early intervention work can address economic abuse, since increasing awareness of tactics used to introduce economic control may serve to limit the range of negative impacts associated with economic abuse outlined at the end of Chapter Two.

6. Specialist Services

Local specialist domestic abuse services are essential in supporting victim-survivors and meeting their needs. This includes the work of 'by and for' led services for black and minoritised, disabled and lesbian, bisexual and transgender women. As Chapter Two touched on, the risk led model to domestic abuse has, to a large extent, limited the breadth of interventions available (see also STADA, 2020) including in relation to economic advocacy and the provision of schemes such as flexible funding.

Increasingly it is understood that more traditional forms of support are not accessible for all victim-survivors and a different approach needs to be taken (STADA, 2020). Co-located services, for example, have the potential to reach broader groups, whilst simultaneously improving the response of public and private sector organisations to economic abuse, for instance, through co-locating specialist domestic abuse services in job centres or within the customer vulnerability teams of banks and utility companies (see Chapter Five).

7. Representation

For the CCR to work, it is essential that people from the right organisations working at the right level can participate, bringing appropriate skills, resources and influence (STADA, 2020). As discussed above, effective responses to economic abuse requires the involvement of 'non-traditional' stakeholders such as money/debt advice agencies and banks/building societies with staff attending who can make systems-level changes.

8. Resources

For public sector organisations and non-governmental organisations, funding pressures can create a challenge – particularly in relation to their ability to be strategic in approach and ensure that domestic abuse services meet the needs of everyone, particularly victim-survivors who have no recourse to public funds. The broadening out of membership to the private sector not only has the potential to diversify funding streams, but also harness more 'in kind' assets such as people, passion and drive.

9. Coordination

Coordination is about systematic and collective activity designed to make victim-survivors and their children safe and hold perpetrators to account (STADA, 2020). As reflected above, a shared objective is vital if each partner within the CCR is to play their role. There may be some challenges specific to non-traditional stakeholders in relation to information-sharing, for example. As such, it may be necessary to give agencies and partners time and resources to address and mitigate for any coordination issues to improve joint working (STADA, 2020).

10. Training

Another integral component of the CCR is training so that partners share the same understanding of the dynamics of domestic abuse. Very few professionals will have had training specifically on economic abuse (SEA, 2017), yet given that it is now named within the statutory definition of domestic abuse this will need to be incorporated. As described above, spotting the signs of economic abuse in a range of different contexts is vital. The consequences of not recognising and/or responding to economic abuse means that opportunities for early intervention may be lost and victim-survivors may be disbelieved, dismissed and/or blamed. This can lead to increased risk of harm (STADA, 2020).

It is vital that training is intersectional in approach and 'trauma-informed' so that responses incorporate principles of safety, collaboration, empowerment, choice and trustworthiness (STADA, 2020). Again, multi-agency training can create an opportunity for partnership working and strengthened inter-agency coordination.

11. Data

Data are essential to deliver an effective CCR (STADA, 2020). Data collection and analysis give partners the information they need to keep track of trends, develop insights and address issues arising. It can inform research, making the case for change and ensuring resources are used to the greatest effect. Currently, few organisations systematically screen for economic abuse, making it difficult to evidence the need to address it.

12. Policies and Processes

STADA (2020) states that ideally there will be an overarching policy for the partnership and a separate policy and associated procedures for each organisation involved in the CCR. This will offer a framework for staff to know what they can do for each other and for victim-survivors. Procedures should consider the needs of the victim-survivor as well as the abuser from the start to the end of their journey and set out what staff need to do to ensure this is seamless. Safety must be central be at the heart of a procedure, giving consideration to the risks associated with perpetrators becoming aware of victim-survivors accessing support in relation to domestic abuse.

Best Practice Example One: Developing a CCR Approach that Embeds Economic Abuse (SEA, 2020).

> Between 2015 and 2018, the London Borough of Hammersmith and Fulham, the Royal Borough of Kensington and Chelsea and the City of Westminster worked together to deliver a Shared Services VAWG Strategy. The multi-agency partnership adopted the CCR model and worked to the UN's definition of violence against women which recognises economic abuse. As such, one of the outcomes set by the partnership was that survivors should receive a response that secured their 'health, social and economic wellbeing for the short and long-term'.
>
> SEA approached 10 specialist organisations within the partnership, asking them to engage with work to scope out the level of economic advocacy provided to survivors and to identify how promising practice

from the USA might be adapted to the UK context. Nine of the organisations work together under the Angelou Project to provide direct support to survivors of domestic and sexual violence (ADVANCE, African Women's Care, Al Hasaniya, Domestic Violence Intervention Project; Galop; Hestia; Solace Women's Aid, Women and Girls Network and Woman's Trust) whilst STADA oversees the CCR. It does this through reviewing the performance of local agencies (statutory and voluntary), identifying gaps and supporting them to improve. SEA's work provided an opportunity to broaden engagement to include non-traditional stakeholders.

SEA jointly employed a debt and benefit specialist with MAP. The specialist was a resource to all project partners. She provided training on economic abuse for caseworkers as well as local money and debt advice agencies. She also delivered casework to women accessing support from Solace Women's Aid and ran awareness-raising sessions for women accessing support from ADVANCE. Part of her work involved introducing services to a screening tool for economic abuse. Over a three-year period, it was established that 95% of domestic abuse survivors experienced economic abuse and that 60% of them had been coerced into debt.

When the three-year strategy came to an end in 2018, consultation with survivors identified that more needed to be done to 'understand coercive control and economic abuse'. The VAWG Strategic Lead actively involved SEA in the development of a refreshed strategy and drew on the pilot findings to develop a picture of the existing service offer.

Following an evaluation, three aspects of SEA's work were identified as supportive in the development of a CCR approach that embeds economic abuse. These included:

- *Providing a level of expertise around economic abuse which enabled the partnership to embed a shared understanding.*

The VAWG Strategic Lead reported that one of the benefits of the work on economic advocacy was that it had brought the expertise needed to respond to economic abuse across the pilot area. She also stated that the pilot had informed thinking around how responses to economic abuse fit into the CCR:

'What was really brilliant about this project was that it gave us the space to take a step back and really look at how economic abuse is being experienced by victim-survivors in the boroughs ... it was looking at the frontline, but it was also looking at that wider, systemic framework'.

The VAWG Strategic Lead reported that she had also seen an increased understanding and awareness of economic abuse reflected in the work of specialist VAWG services in the pilot area.

- *Focussing the partnership on the intersectionality of economic abuse and the way it can impact different groups of women.*

More feedback included that the project had allowed for a greater focus on intersectionality, through understanding that economic abuse can impact victims of all socio-economic groups. This was felt to be particularly important in relation to the differing demographics of the three boroughs.

- *Contributing to the learning around economic abuse and risk through the participation in DHRs*

In addition to survivor feedback and the work of SEA, economic abuse was an issue identified within several DHRs which took place during the pilot period. SEA advised on these reviews, meaning that the charity's expertise fed directly into the subsequent action plans and economic abuse was placed much more centrally.

'To have that additional understanding of economic abuse and how it plays out and how it can be identified really enabled us to develop an action plan that focused economic abuse which, I don't know whether it would have [previously]'.

In addition, STADA spoke about how the pilot had helped increase understanding and open-up conversations between the spheres of domestic abuse and money and debt advice. It was also reported that it had contributed to a raised awareness of economic

> abuse in the work STADA does around MARACs. The pilot was praised for offering guidance and creating tools for organisations, and the conversation kit (see chapter four) designed to support the screening tool was described as a 'gamechanger' in that it had created a new way of speaking about the issue.

SUMMARY

This chapter has explored the potential of the CCR model to address economic abuse through embracing 'non-traditional' stakeholders and sectors that have, up until now, been viewed as part of the 'wider support sector'. This is vital if the CCR is to maximise spaces within which victim-survivors can speak out, ensure that they are supported and hold abusers to account.

The chapter has also considered how responding to economic abuse can be integrated into the component parts that underpin the CCR. There may be some challenges specific to bringing 'non-traditional' stakeholders onboard – for example, in relation to information-sharing. Certainly, some components will be easier to adopt than others. Yet, as the next chapter will illustrate, money and debt advice agencies as well as banks and building societies are already starting to adapt their practice to be consistent with this way of working, leading to positive outcomes for victim-survivors. The next chapter explores the role of different sectors and stakeholders in more detail.

NOTES

1. Robinson (2006) has even gone as far as to claim that MARACs are not part of, but are, the CCR in England and Wales. This is

contested. Coy and Kelly (2011) argue that the CCR model was intended to shift emphasis from victim to perpetrator, from the individual to the community. MARACs, in contrast, focus on a small group of women designated high risk, skewing responses and resource allocation in a way that is fundamentally at odds with the Duluth model (see more on this in Chapter Four).

2. Equality Act 2010 (legislation.gov.uk).

Chapter Four

PRACTICE RESPONSES TO ECONOMIC ABUSE

This chapter begins by exploring what economic advocacy is and how its principles can be used to increase a victim-survivors' economic space for action, thereby restoring or creating economic security/safety. These principles are considered within a continuum of advocacy which extends from individual through to institutional. Stakeholder responses within the voluntary, public and private sectors are then considered through this lens, and examples are used to illustrate best practice. For each stakeholder, the link to economic abuse is outlined and practice suggestions are made.

Although this section cannot and does not seek to provide an exhaustive list of all stakeholders (there are many), the approaches and interventions used by stakeholders in one context can be 'borrowed' and adapted for use in others. For instance, a utility or telecommunications company, as well as a financial capability or student support service will benefit from the section on debt. Taken as a whole, this chapter therefore also provides insight into how a range of stakeholders need to contribute to the CCR (Chapter Three) for it to be successful.

ECONOMIC ADVOCACY PRINCIPLES

To create or restore economic security and safety for a victim-survivor, advocacy efforts need to focus on increasing their economic space for action. This can be achieved via:

1. Maximising access to and control over economic resources, including through minimising expenses; whilst also

2. Removing opportunities for an abuser to continue to exert control via joint economic resources (Shoener & Sussman, 2014).

As reflected in the previous chapter, advocacy work needs to be led by the victim-survivor. It needs to consider both the physical safety risks posed by the abuser as well as the risks linked to the survivor's life circumstances – the systems of discrimination that restrict equal options to economic security and safety.[1] The importance of intersectionality as a key component of CCRs to domestic – including economic – abuse is outlined in Chapters Two and Three. For this reason, demographic data need to be collected across all interventions.

Also of importance, is centreing the victim-survivors' long-term plans as well as current needs (see Shoener & Sussman, 2014). A scoping study undertaken by SEA (2017) found that certain outcomes will have a negative outcome for women with insecure immigration status; women who want to sponsor a family member into the UK; women who want to resume/pursue a career in the financial services sector; and women who intend to apply for credit in the future and want to repair their credit rating accordingly.

A CONTINUUM OF ADVOCACY

If professionals within an organisation do not understand what economic abuse is and are unable to recognise signs of economic abuse in the context within which they work, then they will be unable to respond effectively. Professionals may also be prevented from responding when organisational policies, procedures or processes serve to limit the victim-survivor's economic space for action and/or facilitate the abuser's control. When an organisation recognises that challenging economic abuse is integral to its purpose then it will have to adapt policies, procedures and processes accordingly. However, in some cases, this will not be possible when policies are dictated by industry/regulatory guidelines and rules. Changes to these may, in turn, be thwarted if they are set out in national policy/legislation. This reflects what Sharp-Jeffs (2021b) calls a continuum of advocacy – increasing economic space for action through undertaking individual advocacy and where barriers to safety exist, undertaking institutional advocacy at the organisational, industry/regulatory and policy/legislative levels to influence the systems change needed.

COMMON TO ALL STAKEHOLDERS

The economic advocacy principles outlined above are a thread common to all stakeholders but will look different in different contexts. However, all stakeholders as a minimum should have their own policy on economic abuse which requires them to be trained to hold a clear and consistent understanding of economic abuse, be able to recognise relevant signs of economic control, respond with empathy to the victim-survivor, protect their confidentiality and be able to routinely signpost to specialist support, including to 'by and for' services that meet the diverse needs of all victim-survivors, at both local and national levels.

VOLUNTARY SECTOR

Domestic Abuse Services

Studies consistently indicate that anywhere between 43% and 99% of women experience economic abuse within the context of domestic violence (Sharp, 2008). National Standards for domestic violence services recognise the importance of supporting women to achieve financial stability and independence (Women's Aid, 2015) and outcome measurement frameworks for domestic violence services are increasingly addressing the issue of financial abuse (Big Lottery Fund, 2016).

As the previous chapters have highlighted, victim-survivors will not always recognise and name control over their economic resources as abuse unless they are asked about it. Systematically screening for economic abuse will enable domestic abuse services to recognise and validate their experience, whilst also measuring prevalence and developing an insight into support needs arising for victim-survivors. Services report that economic abuse is more likely to be identified in casework rather than via helplines with their emphasis on immediate safety (SEA, 2020).

SEA has developed a screening tool which is based on the Scale for Economic Abuse (SEA) developed by Adams et al. (2008) and a conversation kit which enables a support worker to frame the questions within the tool. This is important since a pilot with victim-survivors identified the importance of 'setting the scene' when asking about the different forms economic abuse takes. For instance, a victim-survivor might say no to the question, 'Did your ex-partner decide how you could spend money, rather than letting you spend it how you saw fit?' if the abuser did not, for example, create a shopping list that they had to stick to. However, if the abuser criticised a purchase, showed another form of negative reaction or created a negative repercussion when they did not approve of a purchase, this might have led the victim-survivor to alter their spending behaviour accordingly.

An evaluation of the tool further showed that its use, along with the conversation kit, can upskill frontline professionals and give them the confidence to start 'unpicking' experiences of economic abuse, recognising issues that they might not have otherwise. The tool helps professionals think about the different forms economic abuse can take. For instance, a woman whose partner refuses to contribute towards economic costs but who has her own income and access to it will present differently and have different support needs to a woman who is totally economically dependent. It is, however, essential that this work is underpinned by specialist training on economic abuse and that there is capacity within the service to work with the victim-survivor to develop an economic safety plan which integrates physical safety considerations.

Another way in which economic abuse can be probed for is within the (DASH) risk identification, assessment and management model when the question about financial issues is asked. Use of the 'Severity of Abuse Grid' which was developed by SafeLives for use alongside the Risk Identification Checklist (RIC) provides another opportunity to explore this issue since 'controlling access to money' is listed under the moderate risk classification within the category of jealous or controlling behaviour. Different forms of economic abuse can also be uncovered via financial difficulties linked to rent arrears, accessing benefits or debt.

It is also important to integrate an understanding of the dynamics and impacts of economic abuse into the way the service operates. This may include putting in place a hardship fund so that women can, for example, afford travel, childcare and mobile phone top-up costs which are needed for them to access support (SEA, 2017). Other activities could include employing benefit advisors, administering a grants scheme and setting up financial capability, employability and economic empowerment schemes.

In a study which evaluated refuge services, Grasley, Richardson, and Harris (2000) found evidence to suggest that women seeking shelter in refuges may experience more economic disadvantage compared to other abused women (see also Coutts, 2017). When the SEA charity was founded in 2017, many of the women who got in touch had tried, unsuccessfully, to access community domestic abuse services for support in relation to economic abuse. There were several reasons why support was unavailable to them (as outlined in Chapter Three), but one factor was linked to the economic resources that they were able to access via formal and informal social networks. This meant they were not 'destitute enough' to access support (SEA, 2017). For instance, a homeless woman with no family and friends who can accommodate her may end up street homeless, whereas a homeless woman with more social capital might be able to sofa-surf instead (see Case Study Ten).

Paradoxically, the way in which the welfare system works encourages women to become destitute to access the support they need. Many working women accessing refuge accommodation must give up their jobs due to the cost of rent in refuges. In addition, some have capital 'trapped' in assets such as property that prohibit them from accessing legal aid (see below). Such considerations are linked to socio-economic status which is not routinely considered in an intersectional response to domestic abuse.

Money and Debt Advice

Data collected by SEA consistently show that 95% of victim-survivors experiencing financial problems have experienced economic abuse. Sixty per cent of these victim-survivors have also been coerced into debt, so support needs in relation to this are common. On average, a victim-survivor has an average debt of £4,500 with five different creditors, although debts may run into tens if not hundreds of thousands of pounds, with multiple creditors – 27 in one case captured within a SEA evaluation (SEA, 2020). Close to half (44%) of the debt in this evaluation was priority debt, meaning that victim-survivors were at risk of being made homeless or having their utilities cut off.

As Chapter One outlined, generating debt for which their partners are liable is well recognised as a control tactic in cases of economic abuse. Littwin (2012) uses the term coerced debt to describe 'all non-consensual, credit-related transactions' that occur in the context of IPV:

- Coerced debt through fraud is relatively easy to commit since consumer credit systems depend on personal information. Although the types of information required are effective in preventing fraud by strangers, intimate partners are familiar with the information that is required to verify consumers' identities and to make online credit applications (Littwin, 2012). Victim-survivors also report that their male partners forged their signature (Dawson, 2007; Kelly et al., 2014; Littwin, 2012) or, in some cases, took female relatives or friends with them to financial institutions to pose as them (Littwin, 2012).

- Coerced debt through force includes all financial transactions that the victim-survivor is told to make in a context where there are negative consequences for non-compliance (Littwin, 2012). A scenario here may be the abuser forcing their partner through actual or threatened negative consequences to sign a financial document against her will (Littwin, 2012).

- Coerced debt through misinformation is when victims sign financial documents without knowing their true content; this includes not letting them read the document or the document being in a different language. Abusers might also ask for consent to use a partner's credit card up to a certain limit but then continue to use it (Littwin, 2012).

- Debt can arise through unpaid bills. The abuser may steal the money that their partner planned to use to pay the bills (Postmus et al., 2012a; Wilcox, 2006) or claim to have paid, but not done so (Adams et al., 2008). Bills may also be left unpaid because the victim-survivor is frightened to tell the abuser there is not enough money to pay them (Barron, 2012).

- Debt can arise through the victim-survivor having to buy the abuser gifts/treats to appease him (Barron, 2012).

- Debt can arise when getting into debt or taking out credit is the only source of income available for survival, to pay for necessities such as food and clothing or essential bills such as gas and electricity (Sharp, 2008; Wilcox, 2006).

- Debt can arise post-separation since the abuser may also refuse to remove their partner's name from telephone and utility accounts and then run up high bills for which she is then solely liable (Littwin, 2012; Sharp, 2008).

Not only might existing debts 'endure beyond the life of the intimate partnership' (Branigan, 2004, p. 27), but if they are joint debts then abusers are able to continue to exert control since there is no legal recourse to sever joint liability. One party is generally unable to alter the contract details without the other party's consent so the abuser may withhold consent to his partner entering into a hardship agreement or dividing a debt. This may be the case even when the victim-survivor is willing to assume responsibility for the entire joint debt to avoid further contact with the abuser and/or to avoid getting a negative credit rating (Smallwood, 2015). This propels victims-survivors into what Smallwood (2015, p. 28) calls a 'financial limbo' where they have no power to deal with joint debts and regain financial control. If the perpetrator does not pay their share, then providers may still pursue the victim-survivor for the whole amount.

Paying back debt creates a financial obligation which absorbs available income to leave an abuser and live independently. The problem of coerced debt therefore has the potential to undermine women's safety (Chapter One), including when it is linked to credit damage which may then act as a barrier for domestic violence survivors to rebuild their lives. For example, the abuser may also engage in controlling behaviours in relation to the debt. These may include concealing the extent of the debt or refusing to let their partner pay on time, if at all. A bad credit score may prevent a victim-survivor from being employed in some industries (such as financial services), rent or buy a home or set up utilities (Sharp-Jeffs, 2015a).

> **CASE STUDY EIGHT**: Rosie's Story – Coerced Debt.
>
> I was only 19 when I met my ex and had never heard of domestic violence. I was a very confident, outgoing, and bubbly person but I wasn't very confident when it came to my physical appearance. When he came along, I felt lucky that someone was willing to call me his girlfriend. When he started questioning me constantly on where I was, who I was with and accusing me of cheating on him, it was all disguised as love. I was told he just cared about me, that's why he wanted to know all of these things.
>
> I was studying at college at the time, we were living in a different place, and I would commute back to my hometown to see him. But when I was at college, he would be on the phone constantly. I remember one time I was at the train station with my friend, and he didn't believe me – he made me put the train guard on and tell him what station we were at. If I was in a car with a friend, he'd say it didn't sound like a car – I'd have to get out and put the phone to the engine. He told me that I couldn't go out with my friends on a night out – I would sit, alone, in my room and if he heard the TV in the background, he would accuse me of having people there.
>
> Within months I was pregnant. He was controlling, then physically violent. He left me responsible for finding work to support us both, even when I was pregnant and looking after our child. During our five years together, I struggled to provide the basics. He was secretive with money, he gambled, he loaned cash to his friends. Throughout our relationship he would demand

my pin codes and cleaned out my bank accounts. He took out loans and store cards in my name.

One day I went to my bank to query some transactions and they told me I was eligible for a £6,000 loan. I wasn't too sure, but he looked at me and asked; 'Why not?' The bank clerk suggested we take a moment alone. We were barely surviving, but he talked me into it. When we got back to the car which was registered in my name, it had a parking ticket. He ripped it up and said: 'We don't need to worry about that now, we're loaded!' He frittered away that £6,000 loan in months. It went so fast and the only thing I got to show for it was our child's first bed.

I was made to feel bad whenever I dared to ask for any money; I was just constantly kept in this poor financial state. And what people don't understand is if you're being abused, you do not feel confident to go into an employer's office and say please 'employ me, I'm employable'. You feel like you have nothing to offer because you have been worn down. So, there are so many factors to economic abuse that are just so damaging. I was kept in a state of confusion, fear, low self-esteem. I was isolated.

When I managed to leave him at the age of 24, he beat me so badly, I required reconstructive surgery. He was put in prison for his violence, but I was left with mountains of debt. When I got out of hospital, the letters started coming in. And it was thousands and thousands and thousands of pounds. I would ring the debt companies and plead with them, but they didn't listen. I got a housing transfer, but I had nothing – no flooring, furniture, no cooking equipment, sheets for curtains. I had no money whatsoever.

> The debt – along with his constant failure to pay regular maintenance for our son is the hardest battle. The economic consequences are with me every single day, a cloud hanging over me. He gets to move on, and I'm caught in this invisible chain pulling me back and dragging me down. Yet I have to move forward. I've recently set up my own business and am trying to raise awareness to help other survivors. When you experience abuse, any kind of abuse, it doesn't ever go away.[2][3]

Even when there is no direct connection between domestic abuse and financial problems, worries about money and debt will overlap with, reinforce and exacerbate abuse and its consequences (Barron, 2012). As Chapter Two illustrated, domestic abuse cannot be separated from women's lesser economic status.

Indicators of economic abuse may, however, arise during a discussion with a woman who has not disclosed domestic violence. For instance, a money/debt advisor may identify potential 'red flags' during a discussion about budgeting. These may include: money being paid into her partner's bank account; bank statements showing that money is only being spent on/by her partner; not knowing how much household bills are or how much her partner earns; stating that the child benefit is 'hers to keep'; conversations about what costs she might be 'liable' for if she leaves her partner; working but never seeming to have any money; and saying things like 'I'm rubbish with money' reflecting the overlap between economic and emotional abuse (SEA, 2017). If economic abuse is not identified or disclosed, then the advice given might, at best inadvertently reinforce these negative messages and suggest actions which are inappropriate and at worst, might affect the victim-survivors safety (Barron, 2012; Sharp-Jeffs, 2018).

Citizen's Advice and large money advice agencies see high numbers of economic abuse cases (Barron, 2012; Citizen's Advice, 2014; Darnell Bradley & Majoribanks, 2017). In 2014, nine in ten advisors within a self-selecting sample at Citizen's Advice stated that they had supported individuals who had experienced financial abuse, including cases where they had been forced to take out credit or where the perpetrator had transferred financial liabilities into the victim's name (Citizen's Advice, 2014).

In 2013, Citizen's Advice launched the ASK Routine Enquiry Programme. This involves training and supporting local Citizen's Advice offices to ask about gender violence and abuse (GVA) when face-to-face clients present unaccompanied with housing, family/relationship, debt or benefit enquiries. An early evaluation of the programme revealed that knowing about domestic abuse helped improve the advice given on debt/reducing debt (Balderson, 2019). At the same time, however, advisors highlighted a range of challenges associated with working on financial abuse cases, due to their increased complexity and challenging nature. These included: more time and support for the client needed; having to consider client safety; needing to work with and refer to other agencies including the police, social services and specialist advice services; helping to establish new independent finances for clients, including, for example, a new bank account; and knowing how to challenge the liability of debts where appropriate and negotiate with creditors both in the public and private sectors.

Some of these challenges can be met through specialist training on economic abuse. However, given the scale and significance of coerced debt and the unique challenges it poses, it is argued that there is a need to move away from locating debt advice services within the 'wider support sector' where they are currently located and into the specialist domestic abuse service support network. This would support domestic abuse services that struggle with the complexity of 'extreme' cases, and which do not hold Financial Conduct Authority (FCA) accreditation to give debt advice (SEA, 2017). It also addresses reports from domestic abuse services about being hesitant to make onward referrals when there are long waiting lists, the response can be variable and the money/debt advice service does not understand the safety and emotional support needs of victim-survivors (Barron, 2012; SEA, 2017). Indeed, an evaluation of an initiative in Scotland (see Best Practice Example Two) found that active methods of embedding advice into services was more effective than the traditional building up of referral links (Scottish Legal Aid Board and Money Advice Service, 2017).

> **BEST PRACTICE EXAMPLE TWO:** Embedding Money/Debt Advice into Domestic Abuse Services (Scottish Legal Aid Board and Money Advice Service, 2017).
>
> In Scotland, five Citizen Advice offices and one housing association partnered with five Women's Aid groups and a Women's Resource Centre under an initiative to develop delivery models of free debt advice to marginalised groups. The different skills that each agency brought to the project blended together to provide clients with the range of support they needed to deal with their situation. Within the domestic abuse partnerships, debt advice workers reported having to take on a broader, more supportive role than would usually be expected of them. Many had to be able to provide advice at a time and place that suited the client. They reported that the work required greater reserves of empathy than might also be the norm and that their roles often blurred into being a 'supporter'.

Another model with positive benefits is creating a bespoke role that integrates economic abuse expertise with a qualification to give accredited debt advice (see below). This is the approach adopted by the national Financial Support Line for victims of domestic abuse and was also piloted within SEA's founding Economic Justice Project.

> **BEST PRACTICE EXAMPLE THREE:** Integrating Specialist Knowledge.
>
> Integrating domestic/economic abuse into the role of a money/debt advisor
>
> The Financial Support Line for victims of domestic abuse is run in partnership between Money Advice Plus (MAP) and SEA alongside a national casework service. This work builds on a telephone advice line piloted by MAP and Women's Aid from April 2010 until 2012 under the former Domestic Abuse, Money, and Education (DAME) Project. The line was established precisely because many domestic abuse services lack the specialist knowledge to provide in-depth money advice and most money advice projects lack expertise in dealing with domestic abuse cases safely.
>
> The new partnership between MAP and SEA brings together expertise in money/debt advice and economic abuse. In this national model, money and debt advisors are trained in domestic abuse broadly and economic abuse specifically. The advisors routinely undertake risk assessments to establish at the outset how best to safely engage with the victim-survivor. This includes establishing whether the abuser is still present, safe contact methods such as the best time to call, what to do if she

needs to get off the phone and whether anyone else has access to her computer/phone or if her mail intercepted. It also safeguards their address and identifying details; for example, making sure these do not appear on publicly available documents such as the insolvency register if a Debt Relief Order (DRO) is made.

Evaluations have shown that responding to queries and delivering casework via the telephone rather than face-to-face is welcomed and in some cases preferred by victim-survivors due to the flexibility it affords (Barron, 2012; see also Adisa, 2020). It also creates consistency for those victim-survivors who must move around the country for their safety. Because the service offers advice on both debts and benefit, it provides a holistic service. This prevents a client having to go through their situation multiple times.

Consistent with Best Practice Example Two, advisors report that the emotional support they provide is just as important as practical support (Barron, 2012). The most recent evaluation states that it is reasonable to assume that the service positively impacts on the emotional wellbeing of those who use it (Adisa, 2020). The service is non-judgmental and does not blame or criticise victim-survivors for getting into debt. This includes recognising that however pressing financial problems might be, these are sometimes lower down the list of priorities for a victim-survivor dealing with multiple issues such as criminal proceedings and providing support for their children. Advisors find that many victim-survivors need more time than general clients to come to terms with their situation and make financial decisions (Barron, 2012). Moreover, this approach leads to victim-survivors reporting positive outcomes that not only include satisfaction with resolved issues, but also restored confidence in managing money as well as money knowledge (Adisa, 2020; Barron, 2012).

Integrating money/debt advice into the role of a specialist advocate

When SEA scoped out economic advocacy activity across three London Boroughs for its founding Economic Justice Project, domestic abuse services were found to be referring complex money/debt cases to the national advice service outlined above which, at the time, was being run solely by MAP with very limited capacity due to inadequate funding (SEA, 2017).

To relieve the pressure on this one national service, SEA and MAP worked together to replicate this national model locally. They created a specialist role, employing and training them jointly. The remit of the specialist was to hold expert knowledge about domestic abuse and money/debt advice, thereby adopting an integrated approach to cases through which economic and physical safety issues could be 'held' simultaneously. The specialist was located at Solace Women's Aid and took referrals from across the pilot area.

She was also tasked with undertaking work to encourage partnership working between domestic abuse services and local money/debt advice charities. Free training on economic abuse was offered to money/debt services in the pilot area to empower them with the knowledge they needed to respond to coerced debt effectively and safely. These included money advisors at Citizen's Advice and Christians Against Poverty.

Solace Women's Aid reported that having the specialist role on site had contributed to an increased

> awareness of what responses could be taken around economic abuse. It also meant that expertise was immediately available if needed (SEA, 2020).
>
> The partnership between MAP and SEA is now twice award-winning. It has led to the development of bespoke resources on debt for victim-survivors of economic abuse (Tools to Thrive) and professionals (Tools to Support) working in both domestic abuse and money/debt advice charities. StepChange and the Money Advice Trust have been trained on economic abuse. StepChange refers complex cases to the national casework service and an e-learning package on economic abuse has been developed with Money Advice Trust (MAT) for debt advisors and creditors through Wiseradviser.

Data collected via a screening tool can help make the case to funders or commissioners if resources are not available to support economic advocacy in this way.

CHALLENGING COERCED DEBT

Victim-survivors have varying needs. Some want to be rid of the debt and never take out credit again, so DROs and bankruptcy may be solutions. Others want to challenge the debt and take steps to repair their credit rating so that they can access credit in the future.

The legal status of coerced debt is complicated and frequently goes unacknowledged by creditors and the courts. Victims-survivors can struggle to access justice because provisions have not been designed in recognition of how this form of abuse occurs. They may, in certain specific circumstances, be able to rely on the statutory offence of fraud. For example, if the abuser uses the victim's credit card without permission, or gains unauthorised access to their personal information, such as their PIN or password, and uses it to incur a debt or other financial obligations in the victim's name.

However, if the individual knowingly gives their partner this information it could be argued that the individual is not taking reasonable care. In cases of economic duress, the courts have made it clear that any threat or illegitimate pressure on a victim to make or alter a contract must come from the 'other party' – that is the person or institution that the contract is with – and not a third party or an outside force. This includes a partner who is a perpetrator of economic abuse. As such, if an abuser uses threats of physical abuse to force a victim into taking out debt, like leasing a car, the courts are unlikely to see this as falling under the economic duress offence as the abuser is a third party.

The same principle applies to misrepresentation where an individual enters into a contract with a credit institution as a result of a false statement made by a third party. Credit institutions are only obliged to take reasonable steps to ensure that a transaction is not entered into under undue influence where one partner seeks to become guarantor for the other's debt. Here, 'reasonable steps' will generally be satisfied if the bank advises an individual to take independent legal advice or meets with them in private to explain the extent of the financial responsibility they are agreeing to take on and the possible consequences of this.

In cases where there are no grounds to challenge coerced debt based on consumer law, domestic abuse and money/debt advice agencies must currently appeal to the goodwill of creditors to make write-offs. Responses are inconsistent, with a success rate of just one in four (SEA, 2020).

A recommendation arising from the Economic Justice Project described in Best Practice Example Three was the development of an Economic Abuse Evidence Form (EAEF).[4] Modelled on the existing Debt and Mental Health Evidence Form, the EAEF is designed to communicate to creditors a victim-survivor's experience of economic abuse and act as a single mechanism through which a debt adviser can verify that their client has experienced economic abuse, ensuring they only need to tell their story once. The EAEF was recommended to the Money and Pensions Service (MaPS) by the Challenge Group Chairs advising on the Implementation of the UK Financial Wellbeing Strategy in light of Covid-19. SEA is now working with MAP to roll it out nationally.

Such an approach must be preferable than victim-survivors paying back debt for years after leaving, constantly reminded of the abuse they have experienced through ongoing financial hardship and direct debits which leave their account every month. For this reason, 'token' payments in cases where a debt is unlikely to be written off are wholly inappropriate in cases of economic abuse.

PUBLIC SECTOR

Welfare Support

Since economic obstacles are a major factor in preventing victim-survivors from leaving an abuser, it is, according to Brandwein (2006, p. 47) 'logical to assume that some ... might turn to the welfare system to provide an alternative source of financial support in order to escape economic dependence on their abusers'. Growing evidence suggests that 'the two issues are inextricably linked'. Davis (1999) concludes that without the minimal safety net provided by recourse to public funds as a last resort, many victim-survivors would be forced to remain in, or return to, dangerous or life-threatening situations. The 'no recourse to public funds' rule is, therefore, highly problematic and discriminatory (see Chapter Two).

Against this background it is vital that the welfare system works well for those who need it. Yet the administration of joint benefit claims via Universal Credit requires couples to nominate a single bank account. The Government argues that this can help them see the effect of their decisions about work on total household income. It further contends that decisions are best made by the family and that few couples manage finances separately. However, this assumes that the payment will be made into a joint account that allows both partners access (Howard, 2018). The Women's Budget Group, EVAW and SEA along with Women's Aid, Refuge and others have, therefore, expressed concern that the single payment can facilitate economic abuse, enabling the abuser to create economic dependency through restricting access to the payment or insecurity by spending it without reference to the family's needs. Whilst 'split' payments are available upon request, this is dangerous for victim-survivors of economic abuse who may face negative repercussions for doing so (Howard & Skipp, 2015). Moreover, the decision is discretionary and temporary.

Many job centres now have a domestic abuse 'lead', and it is vital that they set up strategic level liaison meetings with local specialist domestic abuse services to ensure that claimants are supported (Howard, 2018). This may include establishing procedures to facilitate disclosure at key points in the claim process, for example, separate interviews for each member of a joint claim when meeting with their work coach (Howard & Skipp, 2015). A victim-survivor who is fleeing domestic abuse will need to apply for and set up a new payment which is payable to them, and this may lead to disruption in their access to welfare support, particularly if they also must set up their own bank account. Fast track provisions will be crucial here.

Training on economic abuse for job centre staff is also vital so that they have a full understanding of how an abuser may manipulate professionals and use policies and processes to control their partner. In addition to the problems linked to a single payment of joint claims, victim-survivors can be coerced into financial arrangements that go against their better judgement, including fraudulently claiming benefits (Howard & Skipp, 2015; Kelly et al., 2014; Sharp, 2008). Abusers may also make false allegations about fraud against them (Sharp, 2008). Furthermore, where benefits have conditions attached to them, then it is vital that job centre staff understand other forms of economic control such as actively preventing a victim-survivor from seeking employment and/or sabotaging their efforts to do so (Ariss, Firmin, Meacher, Starmer, & Urwin, 2015).

CHILD SUPPORT/MAINTENANCE

The use of child maintenance payments as a way of exerting ongoing control is another issue that arises in research. Abusers adopt an array of strategies to avoid/minimise payment. These include minimising taxable incomes; converting assets into property; salary sacrifice; voluntarily becoming unemployed; and transferring financial assets into other people's names (Branigan, 2004; Jaffe, 2002). Research by Cameron (2014) found that abusers on a higher income tend to adopt strategies to hide or reduce it to pay minimum child support payments; whereas abusers with lower income are likely to avoid paying altogether.

Kelly et al. (2014) found in their longitudinal study that the abuser withheld child maintenance payments in a quarter of cases. More recent research by Gingerbread and StepChange found that just under half of single parents in their survey on debt had experienced some form of economic abuse by a former partner. They also found that those who had experienced economic abuse were less likely to receive their due maintenance payments: 24% of those who had experienced economic abuse received full maintenance on a regular basis compared to 38% of those who had not (Richardson & Butler, 2021).

Despite often being in desperate financial need, research shows that women who have experienced domestic violence may choose not to pursue child maintenance because of the danger that this may pose to them or their children (Correia, 2000; Davis, 1999; Jaffe, 2002). A DHR published in March 2019 recommended urgent action was needed to improve the Child Maintenance Service (CMS) in this regard, after failing to protect a mother of two young children who was murdered in the street on the way back from the school run by her ex-partner in May 2017. He had repeatedly threatened her life and warned her not to pursue him for child support. Although she had told several staff members at the CMS of the risk to her life, they still reinstated a claim.[5]

Research has also found that demands for child maintenance can act as a catalyst for custody and contact disputes – another reason to explain why some women may choose to trade financial support and the distribution of assets for more protective custody or limited contact (Davis, 1999). Victim-survivors incur financial costs through being repeatedly taken to court for child contact or divorce proceedings (Camilleri et al., 2015; Davis, 1999). Not only do these represent a vehicle for continued control, but protracted cases can go on until a woman's financial resources are exhausted (Fender et al., 2002; Jaffe, 2002).

CHILD POVERTY AND OTHER FORMS OF HARM

Clearly economic abuse deprives the abuser's children and jeopardises their future economic security too. Anecdotal evidence from DHRs suggests that it can lead to the involvement of children's services who may perceive the absence of economic resources such as a winter coat as neglect. The testimonies of young people also suggests that economic deprivation might be a push factor in running away from home and/or experiencing child sexual exploitation (Sharp-Jeffs, 2016b).

CASE STUDY NINE: Tom's Story – The Impact on Children.

'My dad used to hit my mum. He punched her, slapped her, dragged her by her hair down the street. He raped her regularly and the next morning would bring her tea and toast. It went on for years. My older sisters and I would see much of this. I'd be woken late at night by raised voices and know what it meant. I'd rush to the top of the stairs, heart pounding, waiting for it to turn physical – my cue to run downstairs and stand between my parents to calm things down. It usually didn't work.

Three times we escaped to a women's refuge. It was a relief to be away, protected by a giant, reinforced door with double locks. But after a few weeks my dad would get my mum to return. Due to a childhood cancer, she only had one hand and she had four kids, no money, and the only real help on offer was temporary shelter. Things would be quiet for a few days until he snapped again.

We left for good when I was 15. One night I heard my dad attacking my mum in their bedroom, and this time I was able to defend her. I grabbed his neck, pulled

> him off and pinned him to the ground. That was a turning point. Our house was being repossessed, as Dad's inability to deal with money had caught up with us, and it gave us a deadline to get out. With state support we rented a small house.
>
> It troubles me to think of the children going through something similar right now, because the effects are lasting. I became defensive, had trouble trusting others and felt that everything in my life might explode at any moment. The most significant thing was that it made me vulnerable. It left me open to abuse by a teacher at my comprehensive school'.[6]

Police

Research has shown that six in ten successful prosecutions of the offence of CCB involve economic abuse, but that this is not recognised within media reports (Sharp & Learmonth, 2017). Economic abuse in the context of coercive control also increases the risk of homicide (Websdale, 1999). Certainly, the DASH risk identification, assessment and management model prompts police officers to consider whether a victim-survivor is financially dependent on the abuser, or if the abuser has recently lost their job. However, Wire and Myhill (2018) observe that this question is often misinterpreted by police officers and acts most often as a proxy measure for deprivation rather than establishing whether financial control is being exerted. An evaluation also found that police officers ranked financial abuse near bottom in a list of risks by priority.

In a review of the CCB offence in 2021 it was noted that there have been cases of effective prosecutions based on good evidence, which included evidence from banks to show economic abuse, but at the same time, the formulation of economic abuse requires a specific intent to unreasonably control or intimidate, creating difficulties in prosecuting the offence. The review further noted that victims did not always recognise what was happening to them or believe the police would take it seriously, and this was particularly the case for economic abuse. Yet another finding was that getting or keeping the victim on board with the investigation can be difficult, particularly when the victim is financially dependent on the perpetrator (Home Office, 2021). This highlights the importance of efforts to support victim-survivors establish economic independence.

> **BEST PRACTICE EXAMPLE FOUR:** Domestic Abuse Matters Change Programme (SEA, 2021a).
>
> Following the publication of the Domestic Abuse Bill naming economic abuse, the Home Office provided funding to update the police Domestic Abuse Matters Change Programme developed by SafeLives with the College of Policing in 2014 to include economic abuse. Funding was also made available for SafeLives to work with SEA to work in partnership and provide follow on training specifically around the issue of economic abuse. Before the training, just two in ten police officers reported that they had a strong understanding of the tactics that abusers use to economically control victims. Key areas of the training focussed on how to detect economic abuse, how to collect and record evidence and to use existing legislation to prosecute it. This increased to 98% afterwards. Police offers expressed a desire to see the training rolled out more widely.

Housing

Many victim-survivors must flee from their home and so are at risk of becoming homeless, especially if they are unable to stay with family or friends or do not have the funds needed for temporary accommodation. Research shows that 13% of adults applying as homeless cite domestic violence as the direct reason for their application (Pleace, Fitzpatrick, Johnsen, Quilgars, & Sanderson, 2008). Some may enter emergency refuge accommodation, and either be rehoused by the local authority/social landlord or supported to rent/buy privately if they are unable to go back to the home they shared with the abuser. This may lead them to face the additional costs of setting up a new home. Family Action, which provides a grant service to individuals and families in need, estimates that domestic violence is a contributory factor in approximately 35% of all applications for basic household items such as beds, cookers and fridges to replace those left behind (Bell & Kober, 2008). Utility companies also provide charitable funds for customers who are in debt and need to replace items such as washing machines.

Economic abuse has not been widely recognised as driving victim-survivor experiences of housing insecurity. Understanding is, therefore, fundamental to developing and implementing effective housing options and services (Orr, 2020). Arrears are a significant issue across all housing tenures and a potential indicator that someone is experiencing domestic abuse. The impact of not recognising the link with domestic – including economic abuse – can be severe. Victim-survivors may be left with no proof of income, a bad credit history and a lack of references from previous landlords making it almost impossible to meet the basic levels of criteria needed to secure future housing and set up utilities (Correia, 2000). Eviction due to arrears will also mean that a victim-survivor is considered intentionally homeless and hence unable to access accommodation from a local authority (Orr, 2020).

At the same time, the focus of housing interventions within the domestic abuse sector has, until relatively recently, been on emergency refuge accommodation and social housing, perhaps reflecting the fact that many victim-survivors accessing community-based services have few resources available to them. This means that there has been a lack of attention on other housing tenure types, particularly privately owned accommodation where mortgage arrears arising from economic control can lead to repossession.

> ### CASE STUDY TEN: Joy's Story – Privately Owned Housing.
>
> I was homeless and had no access to finances as the money from the sale of the house had been frozen until the financial settlement could be agreed. He had taken all my money from my bank account when I was too ill to notice, and I was the main earner before I became ill. The 'frozen' money counted as savings, although I could not access it. He used the justice system to obstruct and prolong the case and therefore his power continued.
>
> Despite having very limited mobility and needing medical care, I spent two years moving from friends and families homes every two weeks or so. As a professional person, I was subjected to stereotyping of who an abuse victim is. I was treated with disbelief by many organisations that I went to seek help and support from. I received donations of food from family and friends. I was in a worse situation than if I had stayed. Whilst I wasn't being beaten every day I was still at risk for my safety, and I was being psychologically and economically abused.

Research and practice in this area is starting to grow and identifying specific issues linked to mortgages and other debts secured against privately owned property. Orr (2020) writes how mortgage arrears caused by the economic control of an abuser can lead to victim-survivors losing any deposit they might have put into the property and any equity accumulated.

A report by the University of Bristol found that homeowners incurred financial penalties for leaving a privately owned property, reaching hundreds of thousands of pounds (Walker & Hester, 2019). This included costs incurred by victim/survivors in obtaining protective court orders to enable them to stay in their current property, such as an occupation order or non-molestation order. Due to the legal aid means test, many victim-survivors who are in work or own their own home must pay for this protection (see Chapter Five). Without an occupation order it is not possible to access safety measures such as a Sanctuary Scheme if the abuser is a joint tenant or owner.

Legal costs may also arise from divorce and financial settlement proceedings. Homeowners may have to sell their home and are left having to make mortgage repayments on their own until after the property is sold as it is common for the abuser to stop contributing towards the mortgage – if they ever did so. This may also be the case if the abuser remains in the property. The abuser may also do what they can to prolong the sale and, in some cases, destroy the home to sabotage a sale (Sharp, 2008). Refusing to agree to new mortgage terms means that abusers can force an increase in mortgage repayments, leading, in some cases, to repossession.

Victim-survivors in rented accommodation during this time must find enough money to pay for both rent and mortgage payments. It is reported that when some victim-survivors who are homeowners approach their local authority, they are wrongly told that owning a property (and so being seen to have an asset, at least on paper) means that they are ineligible for assistance such as housing benefit or access to a refuge service, denying them a safe place to stay (Orr, 2020). Ensuring that local authority staff are fully trained regarding benefits entitlements and providing access to funds for victim-survivors and their children relocating following domestic abuse would help to address some of these barriers.

> **BEST PRACTICE EXAMPLE FIVE:** The Whole Housing Approach (WHA, 2020).
>
> The Whole Housing Approach (WHA) was inspired by conversations between innovators in the domestic abuse and housing sectors who were improving practices related to housing and domestic abuse and recognised the need to connect their efforts. The National Policy Group for Housing and Domestic Abuse formally endorsed the WHA in 2017.
>
> It was introduced to improve access to safe and stable housing across all tenure types and to create a range of housing options and initiatives tailored for victim-survivors of domestic abuse enabling them to have increased choice about whether to relocate or remain in their existing accommodation. This involves stakeholders working together to consider the long-term economic security of the victim/survivor, as well as managing crisis situations.
>
> *WHA Diagram*
>
> There are 12 components parts of the WHA. The lightly shaded circles represent different forms of accommodation including the three main tenure types (social,

private rented and private ownership) and temporary accommodation settings (refuge services and supported accommodation). The darkly shaded circles are the housing options and initiatives designed to support victim/survivors of domestic abuse and provide the choice of remaining in a property or relocating to new accommodation. Of note in relation to economic abuse is flexible funding as this often drives requests. Flexible funding is a designated funding pot that domestic abuse support workers can access quickly and easily to enable victim/survivors to achieve safe and stable housing. Common referrals are linked to rental arrears or debts – particularly utility bills or council tax.

PRIVATE SECTOR

Banking Services

One of the tactics that arises in much of the research on economic abuse in the UK is abusers denying their partners access to bank accounts (Howard & Skipp, 2015; Sharp; 2008). This may involve being denied access to a joint bank account; and being denied access to their own bank account, for example, because of their partner confiscating their bank card, changing their PIN number (Sharp, 2008) or intercepting post containing details about online logins (Sharp-Jeffs, 2015b). There is little research which explores the specific role of financial institutions in responding to IPV generally and economic abuse specifically. However, as providers of everyday financial products, banks and building societies routinely interact with both victims and perpetrators of economic abuse and have an unrivalled ability to reach and support those experiencing economic abuse whilst also taking action to close down these loopholes (joint financial products and banking systems) through which abusers continue to control their partner, including post-separation (SEA, 2020).

When the research literature does document victim-survivor interaction with financial institutions, there are some positive examples of this working well (see, for example, Sharp-Jeffs, 2015b) but it is more typically focussed on women reporting poor and inconsistent experiences with banks (see, for example Citizen's Advice, 2015; Howard & Skipp, 2015; Refuge, 2008a; Sharp, 2008). Examples generally focus on bank processes. Difficulties include setting up new bank accounts when, in their haste to leave, victim-survivors often leave behind important documents necessary to prove identity (ADP, 2003; Baron, 2012). Indeed, obtaining copies of birth and marriage certificates is, in itself, an additional expense that women who have fled domestic violence often have to incur (Wilcox, 2006). Another problem raised in the literature is banks refusing to recognise PO Box numbers as a confidential address (ADP, 2003; Barron, 2012; Bell & Kober, 2008; Refuge, 2008a); and taking time to agree to the freezing of joint accounts (Citizen's Advice, 2014). Victim-survivors also report that because members of bank staff have low awareness of the difficulties faced by women in this situation, they can be 'unhelpful'. Howard and Skipp (2015) suggest that this may be particularly the case when customers do not fit the 'stereotype' of what an abused women looks like (for example, survivors living in high income households). Another issue raised is being 'passed' from one staff member to another and having to keep on repeating their experience (Sharp-Jeffs, 2015b).

The Cooperative Bank/Refuge 2015 nationally representative survey found that 70% of respondents believe that financial institutions, such as a bank, should help support their customers who are victims of financial abuse. Responses further suggested that practical responses within the banking industry could be combined with prevention work. The survey found that 67% of respondents agreed that financial institutions, such as banks, should help to raise awareness about financial abuse and; that it would be appropriate for a financial institution, such as a bank, to raise awareness and campaign on the issue of financial abuse (Sharp-Jeffs, 2015b).

Over the years, groups have recommended the development of a Code of Practice to guide the banking industry's response to financial abuse (Citizen's Advice, 2015; Howard & Skipp, 2015; Kober & Bell, 2008; Refuge, 2008a; Sharp, 2008; Sharp-Jeffs, 2015b). In 2016, Citizen's Advice, in partnership with the British Bankers' Association (now UK Finance), developed a useful framework to help banks, other creditors and advice providers challenge financial abuse. This included – validate disclosures; protect confidentiality;

offer, signpost or refer to the right source of help; be proactive; help victims to regain control of their financial affairs; offer forbearance and develop and implement a policy (Citizen's Advice/British Bankers Association, 2016). In the same year, the Financial Services Vulnerability Task Force recommended providing further support to victims of financial abuse (British Bankers Association, BBA, 2016).

Therefore, in 2017, UK Finance worked with representatives from charities, victim support groups and government departments, alongside UK Finance's Financial Abuse Project Group and Consumer Advisory Group to develop a voluntary Financial Abuse Code of Practice. Recently updated, the 2021 Financial Abuse Code introduces a number of principles under the five FCA pillars of understanding customers; communications; customer service; skills and capability; and continuous improvement (monitoring and evaluation, and product and service design).[7] In short, it seeks to create some level consistency in the support available for those who need it. It addresses several issues raised within the research literature, such as problems in opening new bank accounts when women are in refuge due to having a PO Box address as well as resolving problems with joint bank accounts (such as closing and securing money). Thirty member firms publicly committed to implementing the voluntary code when it as refreshed in December 2021.

With funding from the Home Office, SEA recruited a banking advocate to support banks and building societies implement the code. The advocate focussed on providing resources for banks, offering training to their staff and providing general advice to their customer support teams via an advice line. Fifteen months after operation, a summative evaluation found that the main issues concerning economic abuse cases involved coerced debt, joint accounts and customer complaint resolution. Over that time, the advocate had supported 5 banks and trained 135 finance professionals. Although many banks have customer vulnerability teams, it was found that this provision is often insufficient on its own to address cases due to the complexity and the lack of knowledge about economic abuse within the wider financial service sector. As such, signing up to the code was just a starting point (Adisa, 2020).

Practice experience suggests that setting up specialist domestic/financial abuse teams within customer vulnerability departments is a positive next step in creating a bank-wide approach (see Best Practice Example Six). This is recognised as good practice by the Financial Conduct Authority (FCA, 2021). It can also lead to the development of infrastructure that enables decisions to be taken outside of policy, such as: a joint bank account being closed without one party's consent; a decision made to grant a mortgage outside of affordability guidelines if a victim-survivor shows they have been meeting existing payments alone; or a victim-survivor being offered forbearance for a coerced debt and the perpetrator being pursued instead.

BEST PRACTICE EXAMPLE SIX: An Example of a Specialist Banking Response.

Yesterday I had a call from the specialist team responding to domestic abuse at the bank. They have been through my personal accounts and refunded twelve months' worth of fees. The lady who I spoke to has given me a direct phone number and within the next five days will be looking at my credit card to see what they can do. I am so pleased; the bank has taken away some of the burden off my shoulders. I could honestly cry with happiness' (Natalie).

Detailed analysis of data and insights undertaken by Portas and Sharp-Jeffs (2021) within a report for the financial services sector based on the '6 Moments that Matter' (developed by Portas, 2020 – see Chapter Two)[8] led Portas (2020) to develop a PEOPLE framework which encourages financial services firms (banks and insurers) to consider responding to economic abuse for both colleagues and customers in relation to:

- Purpose and business strategy.
- Economic abuse principles.
- Openness and transparency.
- Policies, practices and operations.
- Leadership and culture.
- Engagement with survivors.

This framework is structured in a way that brings together the Financial Abuse Code and FCA Guidance with the CCR approach to domestic abuse and economic abuse principles for a person-led, survivor-centred (1) and intersectional (2) approach that is safety-focussed (3), supports coordinated (4) and collaborative (5) approaches.

The importance of this work was reinforced during Covid-19 when the banks and building societies that SEA works shared that customer disclosures of domestic abuse were increasing. In a context where, for many, it was not safe to contact a specialist domestic abuse service, the pandemic illustrated how customer vulnerability teams can offer a vital pathway to support (SEA, 2021a). Local branches of TSB became the first high street bank to offer a safe space for victim-survivors across 290 branches enabling them to phone a helpline, contact a support service or talk to a friend or family member.[ix]

Employers

Interfering with employment is a form of economic abuse in and of itself. An abuser might seek to prevent their partner getting a job and earning an independent income by stopping them from undertaking education or training so that they do not have the qualifications required (Anderson et al., 2003; Postmus et al., 2012a; Tolman, 1989). Raphael (1999) also describes how abusers sabotage their partner's efforts to attend interviews by inflicting visible injuries, turning off the alarm clock so that they are late and refusing to provide childcare.

Other factors involve stopping a partner from keeping a job. These may mirror those used to undermine attempts to find work but might also include: sabotaging their car, threatening and physically restraining them, stealing their car keys and money, refusing to give them a lift, withholding medication, preventing sleep, cutting their hair and hiding their clothes (Brandwein & Filiano, 2000; Brewster, 2003; Howard & Skipp, 2015; Lloyd & Taluc, 1999; Moe & Bell, 2004; Raphael, 1999; Riger, Ahrens, & Blickenstaff, 2001; Sharp, 2008). Additional actions may include turning up at their partner's place of work and harassing them and/or co-workers, or constantly calling them throughout the workday (Lloyd & Taluc, 1999; Raphael, 1999; Riger et al., 2001). The impact of such interference can be severe, including missed workdays, loss of hours and eventually loss of a job (Walby, 2004). Other studies have reported how women are persuaded to given up their employment to work for the perpetrator who then refuses to pay them (Howard & Skipp, 2015; Sharp, 2008). Here, financial sabotage crosses over with financial exploitation and even modern-day slavery.

Practitioners in the field of domestic violence are acutely aware that other barriers that victims of domestic violence may face in maintaining employment can include emotional or physical health problems incurred because of the abuse they have experienced (Chapter Two). For instance, Davis (1999) describes how some women may develop very low self-esteem or may experience fear, anxiety and even post-traumatic stress disorder which can impede concentration, lead to diminished interest in activities and result in a sense of foreshortened future. As Walby (2004) observes, victims of domestic violence may have to take time off from employment to seek help from doctors or lawyers. This can lead to loss of earnings, whilst reduced performance can impact negatively on promotion possibilities (Walby & Allen, 2004).

Safety and employment issues when fleeing an abuser are outlined in Chapter One. In addition to these, some women will face difficulties in getting a job because they cannot risk giving old employers as references for fear that the abuser might discover their new locations. In extreme cases, some women may even change their name (Davis, 1999; Fender et al., 2002). The overall impact for victim-survivors is that they are more likely to have experienced unemployment and to have had more job changes (Lloyd & Taluc, 1999).

Given that victims-survivors will work across a range of sectors (charity, public and private), the role of employers is crucial, particularly for organisations employing staff with publicly facing roles. This is because victim-survivors within the workforce may be required to support customers/clients/service-users who are also experiencing abuse.[10]

The role of employers is increasingly being recognised by the Westminster Government. In late 2020, The Department for Business, Energy and Industrial Strategy (BEIS) ran a consultation as part of a review on 'Support in the workplace for victims of domestic abuse'. The key findings it reached included the need to do the following:

- Raise awareness and understanding of employers about the impact that domestic abuse can have on individuals: all employers to be able to spot the signs of domestic abuse and know how to signpost to specialist services.

- Build and share best practice amongst employers: all employers to have the tools (such as a workplace policy) and resources they need to support their members of staff.

- Recognise the role of employment rights in giving employers and employees the certainty they need: employees may be able to use annual leave or request flexible working in order to take time away from work to deal with the impacts of domestic abuse (BEIS, 2021).

The Westminster Government also launched the Employers Domestic Abuse Covenant (EDAC) which is a pledge by businesses to support women affected by abuse to enter or re-enter the workplace. Employers are invited to sign the covenant and identify opportunities within their businesses for women seeking sustainable employment opportunities.

A workplace response to domestic abuse not only supports victim-survivors but, in line with the CCR, it can hold perpetrators accountable. Most perpetrators will have little or no contact with the police but are far more likely to reveal information about their abuse to people they know, including work colleagues. Ensuring that a domestic abuse

> **BEST PRACTICE EXAMPLE SEVEN:** Economic Support Packages for Employees (SEA, 2021a).
>
> In recognition that working from home during lockdown measures would be an intimidating prospect for victims of domestic abuse, the law firm Linklaters introduced a new policy and package of support. This included the following:
>
> - Emergency accommodation: Three nights' accommodation in a hotel and a daily living expenses allowance.
>
> - Paid leave: Up to 10 days paid leave.
>
> - Emergency assistance fund: A one-off payment of up to £5,000 to support an individual in becoming financially and physically independent from an abuser with no requirement to repay the firm.
>
> - Access to SEA: To provide fully confidential, one-to-one, expert advice to support anyone who needs to fully separate their finances from an abuser.

policy also engages with perpetrators of abuse in a positive, respectful way does not mean excusing the abuse, but it can help to increase safety. Employers have a duty of care towards all their employees. As well as victim-survivors, this includes perpetrators of domestic violence who, through their actions, are damaging their own lives as well as the lives of others (Refuge/Respect, 2010).

SUMMARY

This chapter has explored what individual stakeholders across the voluntary, public and private sectors can do to address economic abuse within the contexts they operate. The clear overlap between them, and common themes arising, provide insight into the importance of a CCR model to domestic abuse which integrates considerations of economic abuse. The examples given have shown how responses must operate along a continuum of economic advocacy (underpinned by principles) which extend from supporting an individual to challenging institutional policies to create change for all. As the concluding chapter will illustrate, there is considerable scope to extend the approaches and interventions highlighted here into other contexts.

NOTES

1. For instance credit, see Paul Lewis.

2. 'I had no job, no savings. I knew he'd destroy me' – the women fighting against economic abuse | Women | The Guardian ANNA MOORE.

3. 'My partner cleared out my bank account and left me thousands in debt' | Marie Claire MARISA JUDITH BURNES AND ?.

4. Based on an idea from Jeanette Hope, MAP.

5. Lack of reforms to Child Maintenance Service leaving women 'fearing for their lives' (inews.co.uk).

6. My dad hit, slapped and raped my mum for years - as her son it affected me for life (telegraph.co.uk).

7. Financial-Abuse-Code-151221-FINAL.pdf (ukfinance.org.uk).

8. Growing up, studying and requalifying; entering and re-entering the workplace; relationships, making up and breaking up; motherhood, becoming a mother/carer; afterlife, planning and entering retirement; ill-health, infirmity and dying.

9. TSB becomes first bank to offer Safe Spaces for victims of domestic abuse | Hestia.

10. Supporting victims of domestic abuse (newstatesman.com).

Chapter Five

FUTURE DIRECTIONS IN RESPONDING TO ECONOMIC ABUSE

This concluding chapter picks up on the themes raised within the book and explores future directions for research, policy and practice.

CREATING MOMENTUM FOR CHANGE

Rediscovering the term 'economic abuse' exposes the many ways in which abusers seek to control their intimate partners. It validates the lived experience of victim-survivors. It reinforces the importance of holding abusers accountable for their behaviour; and it highlights the urgent need to develop effective responses for victim-survivors – both in policy and practice. Through broadening discourse from financial to economic abuse via the Domestic Abuse Act (2021) there is now a framework within which to respond, and increased awareness of this issue has created momentum for change.

FUTURE DIRECTIONS IN RESEARCH

In research, economic abuse is an evolving concept which continues to be redefined and expanded (Sharp-Jeffs, 2021a). An exploration of the evidence base has shown how the definition of economic abuse has moved beyond the mostly restrictive behaviours set out in the Duluth Power and Control Wheel in the 1980s to recognise exploitation and sabotage 40 years later. This reflects the ways in which abusers have had to adapt the tactics they use to control women as economic equality between the sexes has grown (see Littwin, 2012). The 'wearing down of resistance' applies not only to economic (tangible resources), but also personal and social resources (Dutton & Goodman, 2005).

This understanding, in turn, reinforces the importance of developing the evidence base on economic abuse. Since coercive control draws on personalised knowledge of a victim-survivors' resources and vulnerabilities (Stark, 2007; see also Kelly et al., 2014) there is an urgent need for research which explores how economic abuse is experienced by women and men who are subject to multiple oppressions and who are abused by both intimate partners and family members. Only when a gendered and intersectional approach is taken to framing economic control can its impact be truly understood, and responses through policy and practice be more refined. For instance, the significance of class or socio-economic status has been relatively neglected (see below) as have other protected characteristics.

Related issues which have been touched on in this book include romance fraud, predatory marriage, elder abuse, child poverty and child sexual exploitation, as well as forced marriage, other forms of so-called HBV, FGM, adolescent to parent violence and 'cuckooing'. There is a clear need for more research into these issues too – also adopting a structural lens.

Growing the evidence base in this way would also lead to more effective and useful measures of risk which reflect the dynamics of the abuse experienced.

The development of an accurate measure for economic abuse based on a clear definition must be a priority for the Westminster Government. As noted in the introductory chapter, this measure must be objective and capture the multi-faceted nature of economic abuse. Not only must it be clear about who is doing what to whom, but it must also be clear about context.

FUTURE DIRECTIONS IN POLICY

Economic Security at the Centre of Policy Responses to Address VAWG

Women's economic security must be put at the centre of efforts to develop an integrated approach to tackling the issue of domestic abuse and other, often linked, forms of violence against women. If women are to have economic space for action, then policy needs to be aligned with this goal.

The behaviours that sit within the overarching function of economic abuse as a mechanism of control are many, but all can be understood through the constructs of restriction, exploitation and sabotage – under what Thiara and Gill (2010) describe as a 'racial equality approach'. This needs to be clearly reflected in the guidance that sits alongside the definition of economic abuse introduced by the Domestic Abuse Act (2021). It should also be made clear that the use and maintenance of goods and services can also be subject to control in the same way as money or other property – not just in relation to acquiring them as the definition suggests.

As such, a revised working definition is put forward by Sharp-Jeffs (2021a):

> *'Economic abuse' means any behaviour (restriction, exploitation and/or sabotage) that has a substantial adverse effect on B's ability to acquire, use or maintain money or other property, goods, or services.*

Operating with an accurate definition of economic abuse is particularly important given that the CCB offence has been expanded to include forms of economic abuse post-separation too.

Prevention and Early Intervention

Achieving economic equality is vital, but as has been discussed, it is not a simple solution to preventing economic control. Abusers will seek to create economic dependency and insecurity. For this reason, awareness-raising and education is vital so that economic control is recognised in a variety of contexts. Since economic and emotional abuse are thought to proceed physical and sexual abuse, the need for this work is urgent.

The invisibility of economic abuse reflects the difficulty that society still has in talking about both abuse and money. There is scope for schools to do more through the Personal, Social, Health and Economic (PSHE) curriculum as well as Sex and Relationships Education (SRE) which is now a statutory requirement. Young people are new to the worlds of relationships and managing money. Whilst financial capability is, of course, important, so too is understanding how money, finances and other economic resources can be controlled and used as a source of power. Innovative work is taking place in Australia in this regard. For example, a digital toolkit has been co-designed with young people to help them have difficult conversations about finances and relationships.

There is a role for financial institutions to play in education as well, particularly in relation to when couples take out joint financial products. The research suggests that this is a point at which economic control might be taken away from a victim-survivor, alongside other life moments that have an economic aspect to them, such as having children. Financial institutions, for example, can share material about economic abuse as one of a range of issues that might create financial vulnerability at junctures such as setting up a joint bank account, taking out a joint mortgage, arranging a joint life insurance policy, arranging a savings account for a newborn child or taking out and naming a beneficiary in a pension. The same approach can be taken by employers through the provision of staff benefits and maternity policies, etc. (see Portas & Sharp-Jeffs, 2021).

Linked to this is the need to change societal norms around the ownership of economic resources and entitlement to them. These beliefs are deeply rooted and again, according to the research, particularly challenging to change. Ownership of money is still associated with the earning of money reinforcing the importance of Anitha's (2019) call to recognise household/caring tasks, responsibilities and roles which are examples of economic activity, but which are not constructed in the same way as paid work. Increased understanding of the values and attitudes that drive control over economic resources would be valuable in seeking to design educational interventions as well as behaviour-change programmes for abusers. As a society, it is vital that economic control is recognised and challenged, and that myths and stereotypes are addressed so that victim-survivors are not judged and blamed.

Close-down Opportunities to Control

Now that economic abuse is understood as a form of domestic abuse existing policy and legislation must be revisited to reflect this. Statutory agencies as well as other sectors should seek to ensure that the opportunities abusers use to control are removed wherever possible.

The Universal Credit system needs to be reformed so that claimants are supported to be able to access an independent income. This means that joint claims should be made through separate payments as default. Similarly, nobody should be made economically dependent by virtue of their immigration status and, in line with the Istanbul Convention, there should be recourse to public funds for those who need them. The legal aid system also needs to be reformed and the means test removed, so that victim-survivors of economic abuse do not have to pay for their own protection. Furthermore, government should meet child maintenance payments in the event of an absent parent not paying so that they grow up in an environment that is economically secure.

Access to economic resources is vital in case of emergency so that victim-survivors can (re)gain control and make choices. Chapters One and Two explored the ripple effect of economic abuse and a systematic way of addressing the needs of victim-survivors would be to identify where support could be provided at every juncture of their journey whilst recognising that this will not be linear. Emergency funds such as those recently introduced in Australia would enable victim-survivors to leave and rebuild their lives independently.[1]

Chapter One also touched on how victim-survivors need to be able to build back before they can move forward. Yet another area that needs attention is reparation for victims-survivors. The courts can now recognise economic abuse as a form of coercive and controlling behaviour and soon this will be extended to behaviour post-separation. Yet a criminal conviction does not result in the abuser being made to pay back the money taken, replace the economic resource sabotaged or compensate for the harm caused through exploitation. Sharp-Jeffs and Learmonth (2017) have recommended that consideration needs to be given about how to address forms of economic abuse which result in economic costs to the victim in sentencing and possibly criminal injury claims. SEA has also explored whether there might be scope for the Proceeds of Crime Act to be utilised is some way. Similarly, consumer law could be reformed to recognise new understandings in criminal law, for instance, recognition that victim-survivors should not be held liable for debt incurred within the context of coercive control.

Loopholes in legislation mean that the family of victim-survivors who have dementia and who hold Power of Attorney for them are not automatically informed of a change in marital status. Similarly, family members who die intestate, may see an abusive (ex)husband able to exercise ongoing economic control, even after their family member's death. At the same time, abusers convicted for murder/manslaughter are still able to control the joint property of the person whose life they took.

FUTURE DIRECTIONS IN PRACTICE

This new understanding of economic abuse also needs to be translated into practice responses. As the best practice case study in Chapter Three illustrates, there is real scope to achieve this through integrating economic security considerations into the component parts of the CCR model.

DOMESTIC ABUSE SERVICES

Chapter One highlighted that, for too long, economic abuse has been viewed as a 'lesser' form of violence or at the bottom of a hierarchy of harm. Due to funding pressures and commissioning models, domestic abuse services have had little alternative but to focus on reducing immediate risk of physical harm rather than the role economic security plays in preventative work and long-term safety. This needs to change. A review of the research has clearly shown the pivotal role that control over economic resources plays in enabling a victim-survivor to leave and rebuild their life safely.

The research base has also indicated the strong overlap between economic abuse and emotional abuse and that, when experienced within the context of coercive control, this increases the risk of suicide. It is clear from the best practice examples shared in Chapter Four, that any intervention to address economic abuse must concurrently support the emotional wellbeing of victim-survivors.

Increasingly it is further understood that more traditional forms of support are not accessible for all victim-survivors (STADA, 2020). The study undertaken by Grasley et al. (2000) suggested that women in refuges may experience more economic disadvantage and that victim-survivors with higher incomes are less likely to be supported in these spaces (SafeLives, 2016). Healthcare settings are suggested in Chapter Four as being a potential site through which to reach groups of victims who may be less visible; consumer-based settings may also serve the same purpose.

FINANCIAL SERVICES

As this chapter illustrates, the customer vulnerability agenda means that, in many ways, financial services are ahead of statutory services when it comes to responding to aspects of economic abuse. Work being done with creditors around writing off debt and more trauma-informed practice, for example, could and should be adopted within the statutory sector too. The recommendation that the CCR be broadened out to embrace 'non-traditional' stakeholders creates an opportunity for closer collaboration between the public and private sector. This is important since victim-survivors are consumers of both public and private services and, therefore, need a consistent response across both. In fact, consistency is key.

One of the drivers for the Economic Abuse Evidence Form (EAEF) described in Chapter Four was the recognition that customers receive different responses from the same creditor. There is nothing consistent about decision making, with some customers judged to have experienced economic abuse, whilst others are not. In addition to this, receiving a good response from one creditor does not mean that a customer will have a similarly good response from another. Given that, on average, a victim-survivor who has been coerced into debt will have five different creditors this is problematic. It may be that four out of five creditors decide to offer forbearance, but the fifth does not, meaning that overall, the victims-survivor is still not in a position where they can move forward.

Another important issue is the repairing of credit ratings. Again, SEA has explored the potential use of the EAEF as a mechanism that could be used to return credit ratings to the score that the victim-survivor held before meeting the abuser. It is very often the case that tracking the decline of a credit rating over a timeframe can be linked back to the same period that the victim-survivor was being controlled.

Thus, not only must consistency be ensured across different parts of a financial services firm, but there is also a need for consistency across financial services firms as well as credit reference agencies. This can be challenging in the context of financial regulations linked to competition, for example, and information-sharing.

When the needs of a victim-survivor across multiple products is considered then the picture becomes more complicated still. The 2021 Financial Abuse Code encourages firms to think about linked products when supporting a customer; however, in the same way that a customer is likely to have multiple sources of credit, they are also likely to hold financial products with multiple firms. In many ways, an ideal response would require an overarching advice body with (a) expertise across a range of different financial products; (b) knowledge of a customer's needs across their financial life journey; and (c) expertise in domestic/economic abuse (see Portas & Sharp-Jeffs, 2021).

COORDINATION ACROSS SECTORS

An ideal response to economic abuse would coordinate responses across financial services firms and statutory agencies, as well as legal systems. For instance, a decision taken about a particular financial product at one stage of a life journey may have implications in relation to another stage. The example given in Chapter Four (Joy's story) is about deciding to take out a lump sum from a pension and how this then had no bearing on a financial settlement reached later as part of divorce proceedings.

This would suggest that if non-traditional stakeholders are to be able to fully contribute to the CCR, scoping work needs to be undertaken of all the component parts to ensure that the victim-survivor is able to move seamlessly between specialist, statutory and private services, so that they are able to access justice and the abuser is held accountable for their actions across a range of interlinked issues. A quick win in this area would be for orders made by the courts in financial settlement cases, for example, to be consistent with what banks and building societies are able to do in practice. This is a common issue raised by victim-survivors, requiring them to go back to the court, at even more expense, to explain the situation and seek an alternative remedy.

PASSION AND DRIVE

Most important of all when it comes to responding to economic abuse, however, is people with passion and drive (recognised within component eight of the CCR model) to propel research, policy and practice forward. Women and men across a range of sectors have championed the issue of economic abuse and achieved remarkable change in a relatively short period of time. Whilst this chapter has illustrated the size of the challenge ahead and the amount of work there is still to do, it has also shown what is possible and the difference that can be made when working alongside victim-survivors.

> *I refuse to be told that nothing can be done, and I want change for other victims. I know first-hand how devasting the effects of economic abuse can be.*

NOTE

1. New $5000 payment for women fleeing domestic violence (womensagenda.com.au).

REFERENCES

Adams, A. E., & Beeble, M. L. (2019). Intimate partner violence and psychological well-being: Examining the effect of economic abuse on women's quality of life. *Psychology of Violence*, 9(5), 517–525. doi:10.1037/vio0000174

Adams, A., Greeson, M., Littwin, A., & Javorka, M. (2019). The revised Scale of Economic Abuse (SEA2): Development and initial psychometric testing of an updated measure of economic abuse in intimate relationships. *Psychology of Violence*, 10(3), 268–278. doi:10.1037/vio0000174

Adams, A., Sullivan, C., Bybee, D., & Greeson, M. (2008). Development of the scale of economic abuse. *Violence Against Women*, 14(5), 563–587. doi:10.1177/1077801208315529

Adisa, O. (2020, August). *A summative evaluation of the Domestic and Economic Justice Project (DEAP)*. Suffolk: University of Suffolk.

Advice Development Project (ADP). (2003). *Addressing financial needs of women and children experiencing domestic violence: Recommendations for Refuge*, London. Unpublished.

Aguirre, B. E. (1985). Why do they return? Abused wives in shelters. *Social Work*, 30(4), 350–354. http://doi.org/10.1093/sw/30.4.350

Aitken, R., & Munro, V. (2018). *Domestic abuse and suicide – Exploring the links with Refuge's client base and work force*. London: Refuge.

Anderson, K. (2007). Who gets out? Gender as structure and the dissolution of violent heterosexual relationships. *Gender and Society*, 21(2), 173–201. doi.org/10.1177/0891243206298087

Anderson, M. A., Gillig, P. M., Sitaker, M., McCloskey, K., Malloy, K., & Grigsby, N. (2003). "Why doesn't she just leave?" A descriptive study of victim reported impediments to her safety. *Journal of Family Violence*, 18(3), 151–155. doi.org/10.1023/A:1023564404773

Anitha, S. (2019). Understanding economic abuse through an intersectional lens: Financial abuse, control, and exploitation of women's productive and reproductive labor. *Violence Against Women*, 25(15), 1854–1877. doi.org/10.1177/1077801218824050

Anitha, S., & Gill, A. (2009). Coercion, consent and the forced marriage debate in the UK. *Feminist Legal Studies*, 17, 165–184. doi.org/10.1007/s10691-009-9119-4

Ariss, A., Firmin, C., Meacher, M., Starmer, K., & Urwin, R. (2015). *Where's the benefit? An independent inquiry into women and jobseeker's allowance*. London: The Fawcett Society.

British Bankers Association (BBA). (2016). *Improving outcomes for customers in vulnerable circumstances*. London: British Bankers Association.

Baker, V., & Bonnick, H. (2021). Understanding CAPVA: *A rapid literature review on child and adolescent to parent violence and abuse for the Domestic Abuse Commissioner's Office*. London: Domestic Abuse Commissioner/Respect.

Balderson, S. (2019). *Citizens advice: 'ASK routine enquiry in gender-based violence and abuse' Programme independent research evaluation final report*. Lancaster: Lancaster University.

Balzani, M. (2010). Masculinities and violence against women in South Asian communities: Transnational perspectives. In R. Thiara & A. Gill (Eds.), *Violence against women in South Asian Communities: Issues for policy and practice* (pp. 80–101). London: Jessica Kingsley.

Barnes, C., & Mercer, G. (2010). *Exploring disability*. Cambridge: Polity Press.

Barron, J. (2012). *The Domestic Abuse and Money Education Project (DAME), final report*. Bristol: Women's Aid Federation of England.

Barter, C., McCarry, M., Berridge, D., & Evans, K. (2009). *Partner exploitation and violence in teenage intimate relationships*. London: NSPCC.

Begikhani, N., Gill, A. K., & Hague, G. (2015). *Honour-based violence: Experiences and counter strategies in Iraqi Kurdistan and the UK Kurdish diaspora*. Farnham: Ashgate.

Begum, N. (1992). Disabled women and the feminist agenda. *Feminist Review*, 40, 70–84. doi.org/10/1057/fr.1992.6

BEIS. (2021). *Workplace support for victims of domestic abuse: Report from review*. London: Department for Business, Energy & Industrial Strategy.

Bell, K., & Kober, C. (2008). *The financial impact of domestic violence*. London: Family Welfare Association, One Parent Families and Gingerbread.

Big Lottery Fund. (2016). *Review of domestic abuse outcome measurement frameworks*. London: Cordis Bright Limited.

Bows, H. (2015). *A delicate balance: Domestic violence – The police reporting decisions of women aged over 40*. Durham: University of Durham.

Brah, A. (1996). Cartographies of diaspora: Contesting identities. London: Routledge.

Brandwein, R. A. (1999). *Battered women, children and welfare reform*. Thousand Oaks, CA: Sage Publications.

Brandwein, R. A., & Filiano, D. M. (2000). Toward real welfare reform: The voices of battered women. *Affilia, 25*, 224–243. doi.org/10.1177/088610990001500207

Branigan, E. (2004). *His money or our money? Financial abuse of women in intimate partner relationships*. Coburg: Coburg Brunswick Community Legal and Financial Counselling Centre.

Brewster, M. P. (2003). Power and control dynamics in prestalking and stalking situations. *Journal of Family Violence, 18*(4), 207–217. doi.org/10.1023/A:1024064214054

Brownridge, D. A., Tallieu, T. L., Tyler, K. A., Tiwari, A., & Chan, K. I. (2011). *Pregnancy and intimate partner violence: Risk factors, severity and health effects*. Lincoln, NE: University of Nebraska.

Butt, E. (2020). *Know economic abuse: 2020 Report*. The Cooperative Bank/Refuge.

Camilleri, O., Corrie, T., & Moore, S. (2015). *Restoring financial safety: An investigation into economic abuse*. Melbourne: Good Shepherd and Wyndham Legal Service.

Cameron, P. (2014). *Relationship problems and money: Women talk about financial abuse*. West Melbourne: WIRE Women's Information.

Christy, K., Welter, T., Dundon, K., & Bruce, A. (2020). Economic abuse: A subtle but common form of power and control. *Journal of Interpersonal Violence, 9–10*(35), 1–27. doi.org/10.1177/0886260520916264

Chowbey, P. (2017). Women's narratives of economic abuse and financial strategies in Britain and South Asia. *Psychology of Violence*, 7(3), 459–468. doi.org/10.1037/vio0000110

Citizen's Advice. (2014). *Controlling money, controlling lives: Financial abuse in Britain*. Citizen's Advice: London.

Citizen's Advice/British Bankers Association. (2016). *Addressing financial abuse: A framework to help banks, other creditors and advice providers challenge financial abuse in intimate partner relationships*. London: Citizen's Advice.

CPS. (2019). Retrieved from www.cps.gov.uk/legal-guidance/female-genital-mutilation

Correia, A. (2000). *Strategies to expand battered women's economic opportunities*. Pennsylvania, PA: National Resource Centre on Domestic Violence.

Corrie, T., & McGuire, M. (2013). *Economic abuse: Searching for solutions. A spotlight on economic abuse research report*. Good Shepherd Youth & Family Service and Kildonan UnitingCare, Melbourne, Australia.

Council of Europe. (2011). *Convention on preventing and combating violence against women and domestic violence*. Istanbul, 11.V. 2011, Treaty Series No. 210, Council of Europe.

Coutts, L. (2017). Lifting up the issue: Exploring social work responses to economic abuse as a form of intimate partner violence in Sweden. Master thesis in social work. University of Stavanger, Norway.

Coy, M., & Kelly, L. (2011). *Islands in the stream: an evaluation of four London independent domestic violence advocacy schemes*. London: Child and Woman Abuse Studies Unit.

Coy, M., Kelly, L., Foord, J., & Bowstead, J. (2011). Roads to nowhere? Mapping violence against women services. *Violence Against Women*, 17(3), 404–425. doi.org/10.1177/1077801211398637

Crenshaw, K. (1993). Mapping the margins: Intersectionality, identity politics, and violence against women of color. *Stanford Law Review*, 43(6), 1241–1299. doi.org/10.2307/1229039

Crosby, G., Clark, A., Hayes, R., Jones, K., & Lievesley, N. (2008). *The financial abuse of older people: A review from the literature*. London: Centre for Policy on Ageing on behalf of Help the Aged.

DAIP. (1984). Domestic abuse intervention programs. The power and control wheel (The Duluth model). Retrieved from http://www.theduluthmodel.org/training/wheels.html

Darnell Bradley, A., & Majoribanks, D. (2017). *In too deep: An investigation into debt and relationships*. Doncaster: Relate.

Davis, M. F. (1999). The economics of abuse: How violence perpetuates women's poverty. In R. A. Brandwein (Ed.), *Battered women, children and welfare reform* (pp. 17–30). Thousand Oaks, CA: Sage Publications.

Dawson, S. (2007). Survivor centred economic justice. In *7th annual San Diego international Family Justice Center conference*, April 12, San Diego.

Dobash, R. E., & Dobash, R. (1979). *Violence against wives: A case against the patriarchy*. New York, NY: Free Press.

Dobash, R.E., & Dobash, R. P. (1980). Violence Against Wives: A case against the patriarchy. Shepton Mallet: Open Books

Dustin, H. (2016). *Where are we now? 10 year review of Westminster government action to end violence against women and girls*. London: End Violence Against Women (EVAW).

Dutton, M. A., & Goodman, L. A. (2005). Coercion in intimate partner violence: Toward a new conceptualization. *Sex Roles: A Journal of Research*, 52(11–12), 743–756. doi.org/10.1007/s11199-005-4196-6

Earlywhite, M., & Stohl, I. (2005). *In our shoes: The next steps.* Washington, DC: State Coalition Against Domestic Violence.

Fender, L., Holmes, L., & Levy, S. (2002). *Voices of survival: The economic impacts of domestic violence – A blueprint for action.* Boston: Economic Stability Working Group.

Financial Conduct Authority (FCA). (2021). *Guidance for firms on the fair treatment of vulnerable customers, Finalised guidance FG21/1.* London: Financial Conduct Authority.

Fitzgerald, G. (2004). *Hidden voices: Older people's experience of abuse – An analysis of calls to the action on elder abuse helpline.* London: Action on Elder Abuse in association with Help the Aged.

Gill, A. K. (2014). 'All they think about is honour': The murder of Shafilea Ahmed. In A. K. Gill, C. Strange, & K. Roberts (Eds.), *'Honour' killing and violence: Theory, policy and practice* (pp. 177–198). Basingstoke: Palgrave Macmillan.

Glinski, J. (2021). Unpublished thesis, University of Glasgow, Scotland. Retrieved from Post-Separation-Economic-P-and-C-Univesity-of-Glasgow.pdf (theduluthmodel.org)

Grasley, C., Richardson, J., & Harris, R. (2000). *Knowing what we do best: Evaluating shelter services from the perspective of abused women.* Ontario: South-Western Ontario Shelter Association.

Green, B., & Pearce, I. (2002). *The criminalisation of women: The impact and implications of financial abuse.* Sydney: Bankstown Women's Health Centre.

Groves, N., & Thomas, T. (2014). *Domestic violence and criminal justice*. London: Routledge.

Hague, G., Thiara, R., & Magowan, P. (2007). Disabled women and domestic violence: Making the links. London: Women's Aid.

Her Majesty's Inspectorate of Constabulary (HMIC). (2014). *Everyone's business: Improving the police response to domestic abuse*. London: HMIC.

HM Government. (2014). The right to choose: Multi-agency statutory guidance for dealing with forced marriage. Retrieved from HYPERLINK "https://assets.publishing.service.gov.uk/government/uploads/system/uploads/attachment_data/file/322310/HMG_Statutory_Guidance_publication_180614_Final.pdf" HM Government - The Right to Choose: Multi-agency statutory guidance for dealing with forced marriage (publishing.service.gov.uk)

HM Government. (2016). Ending violence against women and girls: Strategy 2016–2020. Retrieved from HYPERLINK "https://www.gov.uk/government/publications/strategy-to-end-violence-against-women-and-girls-2016-to-2020" Strategy to end violence against women and girls: 2016 to 2020 - GOV.UK (www.gov.uk)

HM Government. (2019). Transforming the response to domestic abuse: Consultation response and draft bill. Retrieved from HYPERLINK "https://www.gov.uk/government/publications/domestic-abuse-consultation-response-and-draft-bill" Domestic abuse consultation response and draft bill - GOV.UK (www.gov.uk)

Holder, R. (1999). Pick 'n' mix or replication: The politics and process of adaptation. In M. F. Shepard, & E. L. Pence (Eds.), *Coordinating community responses to domestic violence: Lessons from Duluth and beyond* (pp. 255–271). Thousand Oaks, CA: Sage.

Home Office. (2016). Domestic Homicide Reviews: Key findings from analysis of domestic homicide reviews.

House of Commons. (2008). *Domestic violence, forced marriage and "honour"-based violence: Further government response to the committee's sixth report of session 2007–2008.* Home Affairs Committee.

Home Office. (2005). *Domestic violence: A national report.* London: Home Office.

Home Office. (2013). Domestic homicide reviews: Common themes identified as lessons to be learned. Retrieved from HYPERLINK "https://www.gov.uk/government/publications/domestic-homicide-review-lessons-learned" Domestic homicide reviews: key findings from research - GOV.UK (www.gov.uk)

Home Office. (2015a). Controlling or coercive behaviour in an intimate or family relationship statutory guidance framework. Retrieved from HYPERLINK "https://www.gov.uk/government/publications/statutory-guidance-framework-controlling-or-coercive-behaviour-in-an-intimate-or-family-relationship" Statutory guidance framework: controlling or coercive behaviour in an intimate or family relationship - GOV.UK (www.gov.uk)

Home Office. (2015b). Information guide: Adolescent to parent violence and abuse (APVA). Retrieved from HYPERLINK "https://safelives.org.uk/sites/default/files/resources/HO%20Information%20APVA.pdf" Information guide: adolescent to parent violence (safelives.org.uk)

Home Office. (2021). Review of the controlling or coercive behaviour offence. Retrieved from HYPERLINK "https://www.gov.uk/government/publications/review-of-the-controlling-or-coercive-behaviour-offence" Review of the controlling or coercive behaviour offence - GOV.UK (www.gov.uk)

Home Office/AVA. (2013). Information in local areas on the change to the definition of domestic violence and abuse. Retrieved from HYPERLINK "https://assets.publishing.service.gov.uk/government/uploads/system/uploads/attachment_data/file/142701/guide-on-definition-of-dv.pdf" Information for Local Areas on the change to the Definition of Domestic Violence and Abuse (publishing.service.gov.uk)

Howard, M. (2018). Universal credit and financial abuse: Exploring the links: EVAW, WBG, SEA. Retrieved from HYPERLINK "https://wbg.org.uk/analysis/universal-credit-and-financial-abuse-exploring-the-links/" Universal Credit and financial abuse: exploring the links - Womens Budget Group (wbg.org.uk)

Howard, M., & Skipp, A. (2015). *Unequal, trapped and controlled: Women's experience of financial abuse and potential implications for universal credit*. London: Women's Aid/TUC.

Hunter, C., & Nixon, J. (2012). Introduction: Exploring parent abuse – Building knowledge across disciplines. *Social Policy and Society*, *11*(2), 211–215. doi.org/10.1017/S147474641100056X

Jaffe, P. (2002). *Access denied: The barriers of violence and poverty for abuse women and their children's search for justice and community services after separation*. Atkinson Foundation. London: The Centre for Children & Families in the Justice System.

Kail, A., Blathwayt, I., & Jarvinen, J. (2008). *Hard knock life: Violence against women – A guide for donors*. London: New Philanthropy Capital

Kelly, L. (1988). *Surviving sexual violence*. Cambridge: Polity Press.

Kelly, L. (2003). The wrong debate: Reflections on why force is not the key issue with respect to trafficking women for sexual exploitation. *Feminist Review*, *73*, 139–144. doi.org/10.1057/palgrave.fr.9400086

Kelly, L. (2011). Standing the test of time? Reflections on the concept of the continuum of sexual violence. In J. Brown & S. Walklate (Eds.), *Handbook on sexual violence* (pp. xvii–xxvi). New York, NY: Taylor and Francis.

Kelly, L. (2013). Introduction. In Y. Rehman, L. Kelly, & H. Siddiqui (Eds.), *Moving in the shadows: Violence in the lives of minority women and children* (pp. 1–1). Surrey: Ashgate.

Kelly, L. (2020). *Analysis of SEA survey*. London: Surviving Economic Abuse.

Kelly, L., Sharp, N., & Klein, R. (2014). *Finding the costs of Freedom: How women and children rebuild their lives after domestic violence*. London: Solace Women's Aid and Child and Woman Abuse Studies Unit.

Kelly, L., & Westmarland, N. (2014, April). Time for a rethink – Why the current government definition of domestic violence is a problem. *Trouble and Strife*. Retrieved from HYPERLINK "https://www.troubleandstrife.org/2014/04/time-for-a-rethink-why-the-current-government-definition-of-domestic-violence-is-a-problem/" Time for a rethink – why the current government definition of domestic violence is a problem. – Trouble and Strife

Kelly, L., & Westmarland, N. (2015). *Domestic violence perpetrator programmes: Steps towards change*. Project Mirabal Final Report. London and Durham: London Metropolitan University and Durham University.

LGA and ADASS. (2015). *Adult safeguarding and domestic abuse: A guide to support practitioners and managers.*

London: Local Government Association and Directors of Adult Social Services.

Liberal Democrats. (2009). *Real women*. Policy Papers 91. Liberal Democrats, London. Retrieved from HYPERLINK "https://d3n8a8pro7vhmx.cloudfront.net/libdems/pages/1811/attachments/original/1390823352/91_-_Real_Women.pdf?1390823352" whole doc (d3n8a8pro7vhmx.cloudfront.net)

Littwin, A. (2012). Coerced debt: The role of consumer credit in domestic violence. *California Law Review, 100*(4), 951–1026. doi:10.15779/Z38VR6G

Lloyd, S., & Taluc, N. (1999). The effects of male violence on female employment. *Violence Against Women, 5*, 370–392. doi.org/10.1177.10778019922181275

Lodge, A. (2020). Domestic abuse, suicide and liability for manslaughter: In pursuit of justice for victims. *The Journal of Criminal Law, 84*(4), 273–292. doi.org/10.1177/0022018320940127

Loring, M. T. (1994). *Emotional abuse*. New York, NY: Lexington Books.

Lovett, J., Coy, M., & Kelly, L. (2011). *Coordinated responses to address violence against women and girls*. London: CWASU, London Metropolitan University.

Lundgren, E. (1998). The hand that srikes and comforts: Gender construction and the tension between body and symbol. In R.E. Dobash and R.P. Dobash (Eds.), Rethinking Violence Against Women (pp.169–196). London: Sage.

Lyon, E. (2002). *Welfare and domestic violence against women*. Pennsylvania, PA: National Research Center on Domestic Violence.

Macdonald, F. (2012). *Spotlight on economic abuse: A literature and policy review*. Melbourne: Good Shepherd and Wyndham Legal Service.

Magic, J., & Kelley, P. (2018). *LGBT+ people's experiences of domestic abuse: A report on Galop's domestic abuse advocacy service*. London: Galop.

Mirrlees-Black, C., Mayhew, P., & Percy, A. (1996). *The 1996 British crime survey: England and Wales*. London: Home Office Research and Statistics Directorate.

Moe, A. M., & Bell, M. P. (2004). Abject economics: The effects of battering and violence on women's work and employability. *Violence Against Women, 10*(1), 29–55. doi.org/10.1177/1077801203256016

Myhill, A. (2015). Measuring coercive control: What can we learn from national population surveys?. *Violence Against Women, 21*, 355–375. doi.org/10.1177/1077801214568032

National Union of Students (NUS). (2011). *Hidden marks: A study of women students' experiences of harassment, stalking, violence and sexual assault*. London: National Union of Students.

ONS. (2019). *Homicide in England and Wales: Year ending March 2018*. London: Office for National Statistics.

Orr, S. (2020). *Economic abuse in whole housing approach (WHA) privately owned housing (POH) Toolkit*. London: Domestic Abuse Housing Alliance.

Outlaw, M. (2009). No one type of intimate partner abuse: Exploring physical and non-physical abuse among intimate partners. *Journal of Family Violence, 24*, 263–272. doi.org/10.1007/s10896-009-9228-5

Peled, E., & Krigel, K. (2016). The path to economic independence among survivors of intimate partner violence: A critical review of the literature and courses for action. *Aggression and Violent Behavior, 31*, 127–135. doi.org/10.1016/j.avb.2016.08.005

Pence, E., & Paymar, M. (1986). *Power and control: Tactics of men who batter*. Duluth, MN: Minnesota Program Development Inc.

Pleace, N., Fitzpatrick, S., Johnsen, S., Quilgars, D., & Sanderson, D. (2008). *Statutory homelessness in England: The experience of families and 16–17 year olds*. London: Department for Communities and Local Government.

Portas, J. (2020). *Living a financially resilient life in the UK: The moments that matter in improving women's and all of our financial futures: Insuring women's futures*. London: The Chartered Insurance Institute.

Portas, J., & Sharp-Jeffs, N. (2021). *The economic abuse threat facing girls and women in the UK: 6 moments that matter in the lives of female survivors. A person led approach for the financial services sector in empowering and supporting customers and employees*. London: Surviving Economic Abuse.

Postmus, J., Hoge, G., Breckenridge, J., Sharp-Jeffs, N., & Chung, D. (2018). Economic abuse as an invisible form of domestic violence: A multicountry review. *Trauma, Violence & Abuse*, 21(2), 261–283. doi:10.1177/1524838018764160

Postmus, J. L., Huang, C.-C., & Mathisen-Stylianou, A. (2012a). The impact of physical and economic abuse on maternal mental health and parenting. *Children and Youth Services Review*, 34(9), 1922–1928. doi:10.1016/j.childyouth.2012.06.005

Postmus, J. L., Plummer, S., McMahon, S., Shaanta Murshid, N., & Sung Kim, M. (2012b). Understanding economic abuse in the lives of survivors. *Journal of Interpersonal Violence*, 27(3), 411–430. doi.org/10.1177/0886260511421669

Postmus, J. L., Plummer, S.-B., & Stylianou, A. M. (2016). Measuring economic abuse in the lives of survivors: Revising the scale of economic abuse. *Violence Against Women,* 22(6), 692–703. doi.org/10.1177/1077801215610012

Ptacek, J. (1999). *Battered Women in the Courtroom: The Power of Judicial Responses.* Boston: Northeastern University Press

Radford, L., & Tsutsumi, K. (2004). Globalization and violence against women – Inequalities in risks, responsibilities and blame in the UK and Japan. *Women's Studies International Forum,* 27(1), 1–12. doi.org/10.1016/j.wsif.2003.12.008

Rai, D., & Thiara, R. K. (1997). Redefining spaces: The needs of black women and children and black workers in Women's Aid. Bristol: Women's Aid Federation England.

Raphael, J. (1999). Keeping women poor: How domestic violence prevents women from leaving welfare and entering the world of work. In R. A. Brandwein (Ed.), *Battered women, children and welfare reform* (pp. 31–43). Thousand Oaks, CA: Sage Publications.

Regan, L., Kelly, L., Morris, A., & Dibb, R. (2007). *'If only we'd known': An exploratory study of seven intimate partner homicides in Engleshire.* London: CWASU, London Metropolitan University.

Refuge. (2008a). *Starting in school to end domestic violence: Findings of a YouGov survey to explore young women's understanding and recognition of domestic violence.* London: Refuge.

Refuge. (2008b). *Addressing the financial needs of women and children experiencing domestic violence.* London: Refuge.

Refuge/Respect. (2010). Domestic Violence Resource Manual for Employers (second edition).

Richardson, J., & Butler, A. (2021). *The single parent debt trap*. London: Gingerbread and StepChange.

Riger, S., Ahrens, C., & Blickenstaff, A. (2001). Measuring interference with employment and education reported by women with abusive partners: Preliminary data. In K. D. O'Leary & R. D. Maiuro (Eds.), *Psychological abuse in violent domestic relations* (pp. 119–133). New York, NY: Springer.

Robinson, A. L. (2003). *The Cardiff woman's safety unit: A multi-agency approach to domestic violence*. Cardiff: Cardiff University.

Rowlingson, K. (2006). Living poor to die rich or spending the kids 'inheritance'? Attitudes to Assets and Inheritance in late life. *Journal of Social Policy*, 35(2), 175–192. doi.org/10.1017/S0047279405009475

SafeLives. (2016). A cry for health: Why we must invest in domestic abuse services in hospitals. Retrieved from HYPERLINK "https://safelives.org.uk/cry-for-health" Report: A Cry for Health | Safelives

SafeLives. (2017). Your choice: 'Honour'-based violence, forced marriage and domestic abuse. Retrieved from HYPERLINK "https://safelives.org.uk/sites/default/files/resources/Spotlight%20on%20HBV%20and%20forced%20marriage-web.pdf" Spotlight on HBV and forced marriage-web.pdf (safelives.org.uk)

Samad, Y., & Eade, J. (2002). *Community perceptions of forced marriage*. London: Foreign and Commonwealth Office.

Scottish Legal Aid Board and Money Advice Service. (2017). Reaching marginalised groups: A guidance document for funders and providers of debt advice services. Retrieved from HYPERLINK "https://maps.org.uk/wp-content/uploads/2021/03/reaching-marginalised-groups-report.pdf" Reaching marginalised groups (maps.org.uk)

Shoener, S. J., & Sussman, E. A. (2014). *Building partnerships for economic justice: A report on CSAJ's innovative pilot projects.* Washington, DC: Center for Survivor Agency and Justice.

Sharp, N. (2008). *What's yours is mine – The impact of economic abuse on women and children experiencing domestic violence.* London: Refuge.

Sharp-Jeffs, N. (2015a). *A review of research and policy on financial abuse within intimate partner relationships.* London: CWASU.

Sharp-Jeffs, N. (2015b). *Money matters: Research into the extent and nature of financial abuse within intimate relationships in the UK.* London: The Co-operative Bank/Refuge.

Sharp-Jeffs, N. (2016a). *Supporting survivors of financial abuse: Learning for the UK.* London: Winston Churchill Memorial Trust.

Sharp-Jeffs, N. (2016b). *A lot going on: The links between going missing, forced marriage and child sexual exploitation.* Unpublished thesis, University of Bedfordshire.

Sharp-Jeffs, N. (2018). *Financial capability for survivors of domestic abuse.* London: Surviving Economic Abuse.

Sharp-Jeffs, N. (2021a). Understanding the economics of abuse: An assessment of the economic abuse definition within the Domestic Abuse Bill. *Journal of Gender-based Violence, 5*(1), 163–173.

Sharp-Jeffs, N. (2021b). Supporting survivors of economic abuse: Implementing learning in the UK. Revisiting my WCMT report – 5 years on.

Sharp-Jeffs, N., & Kelly, L. (2016). *Domestic homicide review case analysis.* London: Standing Together Against Domestic Abuse.

Sharp-Jeffs, N., & Learmonth, S. (2017). *Into plain sight: How economic abuse is reflected in successful prosecutions of controlling or coercive behaviour*. London: Surviving Economic Abuse.

Sharp-Jeffs, N., Royal, K., & Gibson, K. (Forthcoming). *Into plain sight 2: How economic abuse is reflected in successful prosecutions of controlling or coercive behaviour*. London: Surviving Economic Abuse.

Shepard, M. (1999). Advocacy for battered women: Implications for a co-ordinated community response. In M. Shepard & E. L. Pence (Eds.), *Co-ordinating community responses to domestic violence* (pp. 1–8). Thousand Oaks, CA: Sage.

Simmons, M., McEwan, T. E., Purcell, R., & Ogloff, J. R. P. (2018). Sixty years of child-to-parent abuse research: What we know and where to go. *Aggression and Violent Behavior*, 38, 31–52. doi.org/10.1016/j.avb.2017.11.001

Singh, S. (1997). *Marriage money: The social shaping of money in marriage and banking*. Sydney: Allen & Unwin.

Singh, S. (2022). *Domestic economic abuse: The violence of money*. New York, NY: Routledge Focus.

Smallwood, E. (2015). *Stepping stones: Legal barriers to economic equality after family violence*. Victoria: Women's Legal Service.

Standing Together Against Domestic Abuse (STADA). (2020). In *search of excellence: A refreshed guide to effective domestic abuse partnership work – The Coordinated Community Response*. London: STADA.

Stanley, N., Chantler, K., & Robbins, R. (2019). Children and domestic homicide. *British Journal of Social Work*, 49(1), 59–76. doi.org/10/1093/bjsw/bcy024

Stark, E. (2007). *Coercive control: How men entrap women in personal life*. Oxford: Oxford University Press.

Stark, E. (2012). Looking beyond domestic violence: Policing coercive control. *Journal of Police Crisis Negotiations*, 12(2), 199–217. doi.org/10.1080/15332586.2012.725016

Stripe, N. (2020). Domestic abuse prevalence and trends, England and Wales: Year ending March 2020. Retrieved from HYPERLINK "https://www.ons.gov.uk/peoplepopulationandcommunity/crimeandjustice/articles/domesticabuseprevalenceandtrendsenglandandwales/yearendingmarch2020" Domestic abuse prevalence and trends, England and Wales - Office for National Statistics (ons.gov.uk)

Surviving Economic Abuse (SEA). (2017). Responding to coerced debt: Consumer advocacy for survivors of economic abuse: A scoping report of activity in the London Borough of Hammersmith and Fulham, the Royal Borough of Kensington and Chelsea and the City of Westminster. Retrieved from HYPERLINK "https://survivingeconomicabuse.org/wp-content/uploads/2021/04/Final-scoping-report-for-Economic-Justice-Project.pdf" Final-scoping-report-for-Economic-Justice-Project.pdf (survivingeconomicabuse.org)

Surviving Economic Abuse (SEA). (2018). Economic abuse is your past, present and future. Retrieved from HYPERLINK "https://survivingeconomicabuse.org/wp-content/uploads/2020/11/SEA-Roundtable-Report-2018-1.pdf" SEA-Roundtable-Report-2018-1.pdf (survivingeconomicabuse.org)

Surviving Economic Abuse (SEA). (2020). Recognising and responding to the scale of coerced debt: Final evaluation of the Economic Justice Project. Retrieved from HYPERLINK "https://survivingeconomicabuse.org/wp-content/uploads/2020/11/SEA-EJP-Evaluation-

Framework_112020-2-2.pdf" SEA-EJP-Evaluation-Framework_112020-2-2.pdf (survivingeconomicabuse.org)

Surviving Economic Abuse (SEA). (2021a). The cost of Covid-19: Economic abuse throughout the pandemic: A call to build economic safety for women and girls. Retrieved from HYPERLINK "https://survivingeconomicabuse.org/about-us/projects-and-policy/the-cost-of-covid-19/" The Cost of Covid-19: Economic abuse and the pandemic - Surviving Economic Abuse

Surviving Economic Abuse (SEA). (2021b). Response to Violence Against Women and Girls (VAWG) strategy 2021 to 2024: call for evidence. Retrieved from HYPERLINK "https://survivingeconomicabuse.org/about-us/projects-and-policy/" Policy and projects - Surviving Economic Abuse

The Children's Society. (2020). *Response to Violence Against Women and Girls (VAWG) strategy 2021 to 2024: Call for evidence*. London: The Children's Society.

Thiara, R., & Gill, A. (2010). *Violence against women in South Asian communities: Issues for policy and practice*. London: Jessica Kingsley.

Thiara, R., & Gill, A. (2012). *Domestic violence, child-contact and post separation violence: issues for South Asian and African Caribbean women and children. A report of findings*. London: University of Warwick/NSPCC/University of Roehampton.

Thomas, S. (2018). *Exposing financial abuse: When money is a weapon*. Tempe, AZ: MAST Publishing House.

Tolman, R. M. (1989). The development of a measure of psychological maltreatment of women by their male partners. *Violence and Victims, 4*(3), 159–177. doi:10.1891/0886-6708.4.3.159

Tuerkheimer, D. (2013). Breakups. *Yale Journal of Law and Feminism, 25*, 51–100.

Turell, S. C. (2000). A descriptive analysis of same-sex relationship violence for a diverse sample. *Journal of Family Violence, 15*(3), 281–293. doi.org/10.1023/A:1007505619577

UN Secretary General. (2006). *In-depth study on all forms of violence against women*. New York, NY: United National General Assembly.

United Nations (UN) General Assembly. (2002). Resolution on the Elimination of Domestic Violence Against Women, 58/147, New York.

US General Accounting Office. (1998). *Domestic violence: Prevalence and implications for employment among welfare recipients*. Washington, DC: US General Accounting Office.

VAWG Sector. (2021). Response to Violence Against Women and Girls (VAWG) strategy 2021 to 2024: Call for evidence. Retrieved from HYPERLINK "https://www.endviolenceagainstwomen.org.uk/wp-content/uploads/Joint-Principles-for-the-VAWG-Strategy-2021-2024-1.pdf" Joint-Principles-for-the-VAWG-Strategy-2021-2024-1.pdf (endviolenceagainstwomen.org.uk)

VonDeLinde, K. C., & Correia, A. (2005). *Economic education programs for battered women: Lessons learned from two settings*. Building Comprehensive Solutions to Domestic Violence. Harrisburg, PA: National Resource Center on Domestic Violence

VonDeLinde, K. C., & Sussman, E. (2017). *Economic coercion and survivor-centered economic advocacy in guidebook on consumer and economic civil legal advocacy for survivors: A comprehensive survivor-centred guide for domestic violence attorneys and legal advocates.* Washington, DC: Center for Survivor Agency and Justice.

Walby, S. (2004). *The cost of domestic violence.* London: Department of Trade and Industry, Women and Equality Unit.

Walby, S. (2016). Ensuring data collection and research: A collection of papers on the Council of Europe convention on preventing and combating violence against women and domestic violence. Retrieved from HYPERLINK "https://rm.coe.int/CoERMPublicCommonSearchServices/DisplayDCTMContent?documentId=0900001680640efc" ES140708_PREMS 204915 GBR 2620 Convention Istanbul Article 11 Web A5.pdf (coe.int)

Walby, S., & Allen, J. (2004). *Domestic violence, sexual assault and stalking: Findings from the British crime survey.* London: Home Office (Research Study 276).

Walker, S.-J., & Hester, M. (2019). Policy evidence summary 4: Justice, housing and domestic abuse, the experiences of homeowners and private renters. Retrieved from HYPERLINK "https://research-information.bris.ac.uk/en/projects/justice-inequality-and-gender-based-violence" Justice, Inequality and Gender Based Violence — University of Bristol

Websdale, N. (1999). *Understanding domestic homicide.* Boston, MA: Northeastern University Press.

Westen, D. (1996). *Psychology: Mind, brain and culture.* Toronto: Wiley Canada.

Westmarland, N. (2015). *Violence against women: Criminological perspectives on men's violences.* New York, NY: Routledge.

Weaver, T. L., Sanders, C. K., Campbell, C. L., & Schnabel, M. (2009). Development and preliminary psychometric evaluation of domestic violence-related financial issue scale (DV-FI). *Journal of Interpersonal Violence*, 24(4), 569–585. doi.org/10.1177/0886260508317176

Westaway, J., & McKay, S. (2007). *Women's financial assets and debts*. London: Fawcett Society.

Whole Housing Domestic Abuse. (2019). A Whole Housing Approach to Domestic Abuse: Pathways to safe and stable housing.

Wiener, C. (2017). Seeing what is 'invisible in plain sight': Policing coercive control. *The Howard Journal of Crime and Justice*, 56(4), 500–515. doi.org/10.1111/hojo.12227

Wilcox, P. (2006). Surviving domestic violence: Gender, poverty and agency. London: Palgrave Macmillan.

Wilson, A. (2010). Charting South Asian women's struggles against gender based violence. In R. Thiara & A. Gill (Eds.), *Violence against women in South Asian communities: Issues for policy and practice* (pp. 55–79). London: Jessica Kingsley.

Wire, J., & Myhill, A. (2018). *Piloting a new approach to domestic abuse frontline risk assessment: Evaluation report*. London: College of Policing.

Women's National Commission. (2003). *Unlocking the secret: Women open the door on domestic violence*. London: Women's National Commission.

World Health Organisation. (2002). *World report on violence and health*. New York, NY: World Health Organisation.

Women's Aid. (2015). *National quality standards for services supporting women and children survivors of domestic violence*. Bristol: Women's Aid Federation of England.

Women's Aid. (2019). *The domestic abuse report 2019: The economics of abuse*. Bristol: Women's Aid.

Yuval-Davis, N. (2006). Intersectionality and feminist politics. *European Journal of Women's Studies*, *13*(3), 193–209. doi.org/10.1177/1350506806065752

YWCA. (2009). Young women and financial abuse. London: YWCA.

INDEX

Adolescent/adult abuse
  forced marriage, 41–42
  HBV, 43
  parent to, 41
Adolescent/Adult-to-Parent Violence and Abuse (APVA), 44–45
Adult family violence (AFV), 13
Advice Development Project (ADP), 9
Advocacy After Fatal Domestic Abuse (AAFDA), 58–59
Age, 86–88
  abuse and, 12
  structural inequalities linked to, 16, 71
Anti-immigration, 43

British Bankers Association (BBA), 154

Caring responsibilities, 78–80
Child
  housing, 147–151
  police, 145–146
  poverty and forms of HARM, 144
  support/maintenance, 142–143
Child Maintenance Service (CMS), 143
Class/socio-economic status, 77–78
Coerced debt, 50, 84, 127–129, 130–132
  challenging, 138–140
Coercive control, 14, 33, 75
Coercive power, 33
Controlling or coercive behaviour (CCB), 6
Cooperative Bank/ Refuge 2015 survey, 76, 79–82, 84–82, 87
Coordinated community response model (CCR model), 16, 103
  to domestic abuse, 104–106

199

'non-traditional' sectors, 108
recognising domestic abuse, 108–119
stakeholders, 108
victim-survivors of economic abuse, 106–108
Coordination, 113
Coordination across sectors, 172–173
Crime Survey for England and Wales (CSEW), 12
Crown Prosecution Service (CPS), 44
Cuckooing, 46, 164–165
Cultural differences approach, 89

Debt and Mental Health Evidence Form, 140
Debt Relief Order (DRO), 136
Degradation, 34
Department for Business, Energy and Industrial Strategy (BEIS), 160
Disability, 85–86
Domestic abuse, 3, 23, 24–25 (*see also* Economic abuse)
CCR to, 104–106
coordination, 113
data, 114
as economic safety issue, 108
intersectionality, 110
policies and processes, 115–119
representation, 112–113
resources, 113
services, 124–127, 170
shared objective, 110–111
specialist services, 112
strategy and leadership, 111–112
structure and governance, 111
survivor voice, 109
training, 114
Domestic Abuse, Money, and Education Project (DAME Project), 135
Domestic abuse, stalking and honour-based violence (DASH), 41
Domestic Abuse Act, 4, 7–8, 23, 39, 67, 163
domestic abuse within, 24–25
economic abuse within, 25, 58–66
Domestic Abuse Matters Change Programme, 146
Domestic Abuse Protection Orders (DAPOs), 12
Domestic and Financial Abuse (DAFA), 156
Domestic homicide reviews (DHRs), 54

Index

Domestic violence, 5, 40, 73
Domestic Violence Forum, 104
Duluth Power and Control Wheel, 2, 14

Economic abuse, 3
  (see *also* Domestic abuse)
  addressing 'ongoing' economic abuse within Domestic Abuse Act, 58–66
  caring responsibilities, 78–80
  close-down opportunities, 168–169
  'cuckooing', 164–165
  dissolving relationships, 80–88
  economic, social and personal resources, 90–91
  impact of economic abuse, 93
  economic security, 93–96
  economic security at centre of policy, 165–166
  emotional/psychological wellbeing, 96–98
  experiencing, 71
  forms of privilege, 72–78
  gendered framing of, 14–15
  holding perpetrators to account, 11–12
  intersectionality, 88–90
  measuring national prevalence, 12–13
  paying attention to social context, 72
  physical health, 98–99
  in policy and legislation, 4–7
  in practice, 9–10
  practice responses to economic abuse, 121–161
  prevention and early intervention, 166–167
  raising awareness, 10–11
  're-discovery' of, 10
  in research, 3–4
  types of relationship, 13–14
  wearing down of resistance, 164
  wearing down resistance, 91–92
Economic Abuse Evidence Form (EAEF), 140, 171
Economic control, 26–27, 28
  economic restriction, 30
  factor analysis, 27
  measuring, 25
  SEA-12 scales, 28–29

substantial adverse effect, 31–33
two-dimensional conceptualisation, 29
Economic dependency and insecurity, 48–54
Economic exploitation, 29
Economic Justice Project, 140
Economic resources, 90–91
Economic restriction, 29
Economic security, 93–96
Elder abuse, 45–48
Emotional/psychological wellbeing, 96–98
Employers, economic abuse experience in, 158–161
Employers Domestic Abuse Covenant (EDAC), 160
'Employment sabotage', 27
End Violence Against Women (EVAW), 9
Equal Credit Opportunity Act, 74
Equal Pay Act, 74
Equalities Act, 110
Ethnicity, 81–84

Factor analysis, 27
Female Genital Mutilation (FGM), 40, 44
Financial abuse (*see* Economic abuse)
Financial Abuse Code of Practice, 155
Financial Conduct Authority (FCA), 134, 155
Financial services, 172–174
Forced marriage, 41–42
'Freeloading', 29

Gender experience, 73
men's experiences, 75–76
trans identity, 76
women's experiences, 73–75
Gender violence and abuse (GVA), 133
Gendered framing of economic abuse, 14–15

Her Majesty's Inspectorate of Constabulary (HMIC), 41
Home Office, 44, 45
'Honour' based violence (HBV), 40, 43
'Household allowance' system, 78
Housing, 147–151

Independent Domestic Violence Advisers (IDVAs), 105
Independent management system, 78–79
Institutional economic abuse, 67–68
Intersectionality, 88–90

Intimate partner violence (IPV), 13
Istanbul Convention, 13, 168

Married Women's Property Act, 74
Men's experiences in economic abuse, 75–76
Money Advice Plus (MAP), 135
Money Advice Trust (MAT), 138
Money and Pensions Service (MaPS), 140
Multi-Agency Risk Assessment Conferences (MARACs), 105

'No recourse to public funds' rule, 141
'Non-traditional' sectors, 108

Office for National Statistics (ONS), 12

Parent to adolescent/adult abuse, 41
forced marriage, 41–42
HBV, 43
Personal, Social, Health and Economic curriculum (PSHE curriculum), 166
Personal resources, 90–91

Physical health, 98–99
'Post-Separation Economic Power and Control', 63, 64
Practice responses to economic abuse
challenging coerced debt, 138–140
child poverty and forms of HARM, 144–151
child support/maintenance, 142–143
continuum of advocacy, 123
economic advocacy, 121
economic advocacy principles, 122
private sector, 152–161
public sector, 140–142
stakeholders, 123–124
voluntary sector, 124–138
Predatory marriage, 54–56
Private sector, 152
banking services, 152–157
employers, 158–161
Privilege, forms of, 72
class/socio-economic status, 77–78
gender, 73–76
Public sector, 140–142

Qualitative research studies, 29
Quality Assurance (QA), 105

Relationships, dissolving, 80
  age, 86–88
  disability, 85–86
  ethnicity, 81–84
  sexuality, 84–85
Risk Identification Checklist (RIC), 125
Romance fraud, 56–58

Schemers, 54–56
Serious Crime Act, 6, 8, 31–32, 67
'Severity of Abuse Grid', 125
Sex and Relationships Education (SRE), 166
Sexuality, 84–85
Shared management system, 78–79
Social context, 72
Social resources, 90–91
Socioeconomic status, 72, 95
'Space for action' concept, 14, 75
Specialist Domestic Violence Courts (SDVCs), 105
Stakeholders, 108
Standing Together Against Domestic Abuse (STADA), 105
Substantial adverse effect, 31–33
'Substantial and adverse effect', 39
Surveillance, 34
Surviving Economic Abuse (SEA), 7, 9

'Targets of control', 23
'Technology' of economic abuse
  Amy's story, 49–50
  Annie's story, 51–53
  APVA, 44–45
  constructs, 25–33
  in context of AFV, 40–41
  within course of conduct, 33–34
  domestic abuse, 24–25
  Domestic Abuse Act, 23
  within Domestic Abuse Act, 58
  economic abuse post-separation, 60–63
  economic dependency and insecurity, 48–54
  economic power and control wheel, 38
  elder abuse, 45–48
  after fatal domestic abuse, 64–66
  FGM, 44
  forms of control, 37–39
  institutional economic abuse, 67–68
  Natalie's story, 35–36

ongoing repercussions of economic abuse, 59–60
parent to adolescent/adult abuse, 41–44
romance fraud, 56–58
schemers, 54–56
as single incident, 39–40
Trans identity, 76
'Trauma-informed' practice, 114, 171

United Nations (UN), 7
Universal Credit system, 168
US General Accounting Office, 97
US Immigration and Nationality Act, 88

Victim-survivors, 138
of economic abuse, 106–108

Violence Against Women and Girls (VAWG), 6
economic security at centre of policy responses to, 165–166
Voluntary sector, 124
domestic abuse services, 124–127
money and debt advice, 127–138

Welfare support, 140–142
Whole Housing Approach (WHA), 150–151
Women's experiences of abuse, 13
of domestic abuse, 86
emotional abuse in, 73–75
financial abuse in, 73–75, 86–87
of intimate violence, 86

www.ingramcontent.com/pod-product-compliance
Lightning Source LLC
Chambersburg PA
CBHW071408300426
44114CB00016B/2229